The Tie That Binds

Other Books By Jeffrey Pedersen

Endless Runnings

River Reflections

Cross-Winter Skiing

Christmas Ponderings

The Tie That Binds

Building a Strong Marriage

Jeffrey Pedersen

Baal Hamon Publishers
Akure   London   New York

© Jeffrey P. Pedersen, 2012.

All rights reserved. No part of this publication may be reproduced, stored in a retrieval system or transmitted in any way by any means, electronic, mechanical, photocopy, recording or otherwise, without the prior permission of the copyright holder except as provided by the Nigeria and International copyright laws. Unless otherwise noted, all scriptures are taken from the Holy Bible, New International Version, Copyright © 1973, 1978, 1984 by the International Bible Society. Used by permission of Zondervan Publishing House. The "NIV" and "New International Version" trademarks are registered in the United States Patent and Trademark Office by International Bible Society.

ISBN-10: 978-49565-2-7
ISBN-13: 978-978-49565-2-9

International Correspondence:
Baal Hamon,
27 Old Gloucester Street,
London,
WC1N 3AX,
England.

www.baalhamonpublishers.com
publishers@baalhamon.com

This book is in memory of Lyle Mellor. He was devoted to his family, country, community, and church.

CONTENTS

Preface ix

1. The Tie That binds 1

2. Communication 13

3. Male & Female 23

4. Love 31

5. The Vow 39

6. Dreams and Goals 51

7. Finances 61

8. Conflict 71

9. Temptation 83

10. Children 95

11. Storms 111

12. Imaging 123

Bibliography 135

PREFACE

The Tie That Binds is a book on marriage. This book will give couples the tools that will build and strengthen their marriages for a lifetime. Couples want a nice wedding ceremony, but what is most important is having a strong marriage that will endure the tests of time. God is the designer and builder of marriage, and wants each couple to experience the blessed joy that his presence brings.

When a couple gets married, I hear people say, "You got hitched." We don't use hitches to unite a couple in marriage. There is a bond that does bind the hearts of couples together, and that is the love of Jesus Christ.

Jesus' love is the tie that binds.

The chapters of this book will help couples work on their marriages. Each chapter will focus on an important marriage topic that will help couples avoid pitfalls that can weaken and destroy their marriage, while developing the skills to nurture a healthy marriage. At the end of each chapter are study questions that will help foster discussion on each topic.

This book can be used by couples who are preparing for marriage, couples who are looking to strengthen their marriage, small group settings, marriage retreats, and marriage care programs at your church.

I rejoice with couples on their wedding day, but my prayer is that each couple will be there for each other at the end when death finally parts them. May God bless your marriage as you read and study this book.

Jeffrey P. Pedersen

1

THE TIE THAT BINDS

"For this reason a man will leave his father and mother and be united to his wife, and they will become one flesh." (Genesis 2:24)

God is the designer and builder of creation. The word "creation" implies a creator, meaning something outside of itself had to create it. All created things are of intelligent design. A car does not just appear in our driveway as a product of a two-billion-year accidental process. The car has a designer and builder. Every part of the car has an important part of the overall working of its mechanical precision. Creation is like the car, it is intricately made by a designer and builder, who is God.

We can place two lumps of clay on a table. A potter works with the one lump of clay, while the other lump of

The Tie That Binds

clay remains untouched. The potter will take the one lump of clay and create many things. The lump of clay that has no potter will remain a lump of clay throughout time.

Creation is to work and serve God's creative purposes. Creation gives glory to God through worship. Worship is how we are in fellowship with God. The beauty of the flowers, the singing of the birds, and the gathering of God's people in the sanctuary, are expressions of worship. Creation pays homage to God, our creator.

Creation serves God's creative purposes. Everything has an important function in the order of God's creation. The seeds, soil, sunshine, rain, animals, plants, rocks and humanity, all have important roles in God's creative plan. God has given a part for humanity to play. God gives the seeds, the soil, the rain, and the sunshine, but has given the farmer the part in sowing and reaping the harvest. God has given the ability for our bodies to heal, but has given the doctor the part of binding the wounds, performing the surgeries, and prescribing the medicine. God has given materials, but has given the carpenter the part of building.

Humanity has fallen to sin. The original sin is the desire to be God, so humanity's nature is now one of rebelliousness against God, and to use creation for self-centered interests. Sin brings a separation between humanity and God, a separation between humanity with itself, and a separation between humanity and creation.

The Tie That Binds

Sin wreaks havoc with God's creative order. As a result of sin, people do not know whom or what to worship, and they misuse the creation that God has blessed them with. Sin changes humanity's attitude from being loving stewards of the earth to having a dominance that brings destruction to creation.

I have a key that was made for the purpose of unlocking my truck's door and starting its engine. Sometimes I will use my key as a box cutter to open packages that I receive in the mail. The key does a good job of opening the boxes, but that was not the purpose for its creation. Like the key, humanity uses creation for purposes other than what God intended. God is creator, and we are the created. God is the owner, and God has called us to be the managers of creation. Creation works best when it is living in harmony with God's created purposes.

Marriage is part of God's creative order. God has established marriage for a husband and wife to live in a loving, committed relationship. Marriage establishes family, allowing for procreation and a nurturing environment for children. Marriage is a foundation for societal order, as it passes Christian values from one generation to the next. A couple worships the Lord as they share in God's love, and they serve God as they minister to the needs of each other, their children, and

The Tie That Binds

their community.

Marriage is defined as a covenant between one man and one woman. A couple exchanges faithful promises to each other and before God that are legally binding.

A man shall leave his parents, as a woman will leave her parents, and they shall be united together as one. The word used to describe this is "cleave". Cleave is a word that has two opposite definitions. Cleave is defined as, "separating." Cleave is also defined as, "uniting." Cleave in its two definitions best describes marriage. There is the "leaving" of his and her parents, and a "uniting" with one's spouse. This doesn't mean that a couple cannot maintain a relationship with their parents and in-laws, but there needs to be a separate identity from them.

I once knew a couple who got married, and the bride insisted that they live with her parents. They would share the same home, eat at the same table, and share in all the traditions of her family. Her mother was a very controlling person. Their marriage did not last, because they failed to make a healthy separation from her parents. They lacked an identity of their own.

It is healthy when a couple can meld the values and traditions of their respective families, and have an identity of their own. God is able to meld couples through his love. It is like taking primary colors and melding them together to form a new color. When we mix the colors red and blue, we get the color purple. God mixes the respective colors of a husband and wife, and gives them a new color.

A husband and wife are to cleave. They are to leave their parents and be united together as one. What bond can unite two people together? There are many strong physical bonds. A rope can tie a ship to its dock. A chain can bond a bike to a rack. A hitch can bond a tractor and trailer together. Glue can bond two pieces of wood together. A weld can bond two pieces of metal together. As strong as these bonds may be, they cannot bring two people together as one. I have been the officiant at many weddings, but never have I welded a couple together. What bond can bring a husband and a wife together? The bond that God uses to bond a husband and wife together is love. Love is the strongest bond that the world has ever known. We are spiritual people. It is God's spirit, the Holy Spirit that bonds our spirits together as one. The strongest bonds are the ones that we cannot see, they are spiritual in nature.

The nature of God's love is that it is eternal. The Apostle Paul writes in 1 Corinthians 13:13, "And now these three remain faith, hope and love. But the greatest of these is love." Love is the greatest because it is everlasting. Love is a gift of heaven that we experience in this world, and we will also experience in heaven. It is this love that sustains marriage for a lifetime. God has established marriage to last until death parts us. A lifetime is not too long to live as a married couple. When we try to bond our marriages with things of this world, rather than God, the marriage doesn't have the strength to withstand the tests of life. When a couple bases their marriage on worldly things, such things cannot hold us in the midst of our changing lives and world. When God is the designer and maker of marriage, we must remember that marriage is a good thing. God doesn't give us things that are impossible to fulfill, but rather, things that are attainable within his creative purposes. Our lives are mortal, but God's love is eternal. It is God's love that will bond and sustain marriage for a lifetime.

The second nature of God's love is that it cannot be destroyed. Not even death could keep the love of God in Jesus Christ in the tomb. The Apostle Paul writes in Romans 8:37-39:

"No, in all these things we are more than conquerors through him who loved us. For I am convinced that neither death nor life, neither angels nor demons, neither the present nor the future, nor any powers, neither height nor depth, nor anything else in all creation, will be able to separate us from the love of God that is in Christ Jesus our Lord."

In metal fabrications class, the students were taught to

weld. The test on welding was not a written one, but rather, the test was to weld two pieces of metal together. They then would put the welded metal into a press. A good weld is stronger than the metal itself. If the metal broke and the weld remained strong, then the student would pass. If the weld broke first then the student would fail. When Jesus is the bond of our marriage, we as an individual may break, but the bond of Jesus' love will never break.

The third nature of God's love is that it grows. Jesus said, "I am the vine, you are the branches. If a man remains in me and I in him, he will bear much fruit; apart from me you can do nothing." (John 15:5) Jesus is the vine that gives all the nurturing love for marriage. As we abide in Jesus, our love continues to grow and branch out in life. As much as a couple loves each other on their wedding day, when they live their lives in Jesus' love, they will love each other more as the years go by. In John chapter 15, Jesus teaches us to remain in his love, remain in his command, and remain in his word (the Bible). In marriage, as we practice what Jesus instructed, our love will continue to grow in marriage until life's end.

It is from love that we get other bonds that are so important in marriage. The Apostle Paul writes in 1 Corinthians 13:4-7:

"Love is patient, love is kind. It does not envy, it does

not boast, it is not proud. It is not rude, it is not self-seeking, it is not easily angered, it keeps no record of wrongs. Love does not delight in evil but rejoices with the truth. It always protects, always trusts, always hopes, always perseveres."

These are all byproducts of love that are so important in marriage. It is out of love that we have the virtuous bonds of patients, kindness, joy, truth, trust, hope, and perseverance.

A question that needs to be asked is: "Are you marrying Jesus?" Jesus would make the perfect spouse, and as the Bible teaches us that Jesus is the bridegroom and we the church are the bride. Our relationship with Jesus is very intimate to where we are called the bride of Christ. We are not married to Jesus, but when a person grows and matures in his relationship with Jesus Christ, he becomes more Christ-like. A person is not married to Jesus, but as a married couple is nurtured in the love of Jesus, they are.

The Apostle Paul writes in Colossians 3:12-14, "Therefore, as God's chosen people, holy and dearly loved, clothe yourselves with compassion, kindness, gentleness and patience. Bear with each other and forgive whatever grievances you may have against one another. Forgive as the lord forgave you. And over all these virtues put on love, which binds them all together in perfect unity."

People look nice on the day of a wedding. They are wearing rented tuxes and beautiful dresses. It is important for a couple to look nice on their wedding day, but it is even more important that the couple is dressed in the way that Paul describes on all the days that follow. When a person is filled with the Holy Spirit, they will be clothed with the virtues of God. These are Christ-like virtues that will make for a strong marriage. This will allow a couple to live in the purpose that God intended for them. When you marry a person who is clothed in the way the Apostle Paul describes, you will be married to a Christ-like person. This person continues to mature and grow into the person that God wants him to be. This is a person who is operating not out of the conditional love of the world, but rather the unconditional love of God. This person has a love of God and has a love for you. This person worships and honors God and will honor you. This person will be of high moral integrity. This person will make it his aim to do the right thing. This person will serve you in sickness and health, be considerate of you, and show kindness. This person will show compassion, understanding, and perseverance in times of struggle. This person will be accountable to God and take his promises very seriously. This is a person who is living his life in accordance to the purpose, life, and marriage which God intended for creation. Your marriage is bonded in the love of God, the love that raised Jesus from the dead. God's love has been poured into our hearts by the Holy Spirit. The Holy Spirit is Jesus' risen presence in us. Jesus' presence will mold and make us to be the people that God intends for us to be.

My definition of a Christian comes from the Apostle Paul's words written in Galatians 2:20, "I have been crucified with Christ and I no longer live, but Christ lives in me." It is the risen Jesus Christ who dwells in the Christian. A believer is full of the salvation life of Jesus. This is also the life that fills and bonds marriages.

A soda pop can, when filled with its contents, is valuable. When the can is emptied of its contents is of no value. We do not want sacred rituals such as: baptism, confirmation, and marriage to be empty formalities that people now pass down from one generation to the next. We do not want marriage to be like an empty pop can. We want marriage to be what God fully purposed and intended for it to be. When Christ fills a marriage, it is full of the most valuable contents, the life of God. When a couple is bonded in God's love, they will live in God's creative purposes for marriage.

STUDY QUESTIONS

1. Is there something about creation that convinces you of divine intelligence?
2. God has created everything to have a purpose according to his plan. What are examples of created things being used for purposes other than what they were intended for?
3. The word "cleave" has its two definitions. What is hard about leaving your parents? What are some of the difficulties of uniting to each other?
4. Love is the bond that God uses to unite us. God's love is eternal and indestructible. What are ways that you nurture God's love in marriage?
5. Are you marrying Jesus? What are Christ-like qualities you see in your spouse?
6. At a wedding, everyone is clothed with beautiful dresses and handsome suits and tuxes. How are you clothed in the virtues of Jesus?

2

COMMUNICATION

In marriage, good communication begins with prayer. Prayer is our communication with God. It is the time spent in prayer that allows God to mold and make us into his people. God's inspiration will influence how we interact with our spouse. Prayer inspires us to be Christ-like in nature. Our time spent with God in prayer will make us loving, patient, kind, compassionate, and looking to the needs of our spouse. The Apostle Paul writes in 1 Thessalonians 5:16-18, "Be joyful always, pray continually, give thanks in all circumstances, for this is God's will for you in Christ Jesus." In marriage, as it is in life, it is important to be joyful in spirit, to have a thankful attitude, and to pray for God's continuing guidance. When a couple prays, they are open to the Holy Spirit's work to bond them, and mold them in a Christian character for their lives. Prayer may not change outward circumstances, but it will always change you. This gives us a Christ-like love and wisdom to face the many circumstances of life that challenge us as couples. As we spend time communicating with God, this will put us in the right frame of mind to communicate with our spouse in the most optimal way.

A tool that will give strength to a married couple is communication. Communication is a miraculous thing; the thoughts of one person's mind can be transferred into the mind of another person. A person who does this well will be a strength to those around him. Think of a person who is in a high position in a company. This person's subordinates may do the work of the company better than he can, but the reason why he is in the high position has to do with his ability to communicate effectively with others. This person understands the whole picture of what the company is all about, and communicates to every person the important role that each one has. When the person in this position is doing a good job of communicating, the whole system functions well. When this person is not an effective communicator, it doesn't take long for the system to break down and there are a lot

Communication

of disgruntled employees.

Communication is important in marriage. When a couple communicates well, they understand each other, they are able to affirm each other, and have a great ability to work through various situations. Good communication prevents a lot of problems in marriage, and when problems come, they are able to work through them before a deeper division is created.

One way that we communicate is nonverbally. What is your spouse communicating with you nonverbally? I once had a dog, and even though it couldn't speak beyond a bark, it was a great communicator through nonverbal communication. I knew when the dog was happy, sad, guilty, in need of something, and it was always able to communicate affection. When we communicate nonverbally, what are we communicating through our eyes, facial expressions, gestures, and posture?

When we ask our spouse, "How are you doing?" and he or she responds by saying, "Just fine", even though the nonverbal communication is telling us otherwise; it is good to say in a loving way, "If you need to talk about it, I will be in the other room."

Our nonverbal communication conveys whether we are sad, angry, guilty, happy, excited, or interested. It is important that our posture, facial expressions, and gestures show an intent interest in our spouse.

The Apostle James writes in James 1:19, "Everyone should be quick to listen, slow to speak and slow to become angry." God gave us two ears and one mouth for a reason. We are to listen at least twice as much as we speak. A good communicator listens well. This is why people are willing to pay professional counselors, because they are trained listeners. A spouse may say, "I like going to the counselor, because he takes the time to listen, and understands me, while my spouse does not."

Who do you appreciate more, someone who constantly speaks without end or someone who listens intently to you? When people listen to us, it communicates an interest, a concern, and a love for us. People who listen value others.

There are five common mistakes that people make when communicating with others. These are listening mistakes that hurt relationships, and hurt marriages.

The first mistake in listening is selfish communication. This is where a person speaks without ever taking into consideration that another person may have something to share also. He sees communication as a one-way street. He has something to say, and everyone else must listen. He communicates to his wife that he is important, and she is not. He is not considerate of her feelings, thoughts, and values on a subject. He is the king on the throne, and she is a subservient who is not allowed to speak. What is

Communication

important is not what we have to say, but listening to what matters to her.

The second mistake in listening is remembrance. When we are listening to someone share her story, she will share something that will remind you of a similar situation that happened to you. At this point, it is easy to barge in and start sharing your similar story. This communicates that her story really isn't all that important. You communicate that your story is far more important than hers. Instead of listening, you have one-upped her in importance. She feels devalued when this happens. In listening to other people's conversations, things that they say will bring to memory many of your own similar experiences. It is important to listen to her experiences.

A third mistake in listening is jumping to hasty conclusions. Listening takes patience to hear a person through. When someone is halfway through sharing his story, it is easy to jump to a conclusion about the rest of the story. I will play a game with people, where I will start sharing a story and at a certain point in the story; I will stop and ask each one to take a few minutes to make up the rest of the story. Each person will use his/her creativity and each one will finish the story differently. When we jump to a hasty conclusion when listening to someone else's story, we will always come to a hasty false conclusion. We need to listen to the whole story, not a percentage of it.

A fourth mistake in listening is when someone is sharing with us, only to have someone else appear in the room that seemingly is more important. At once, we make eye contact with that person, and communicate something to them. Sometimes we will leave the person who is sharing with us, and go to the person who is "more important." When we leave a person in mid-conversation, and start visiting someone more important, it devalues the person. They will be hurt by such actions. It is important to keep good eye contact and listen intently to the other person.

The fifth mistake in listening is divided attention. This is when a man is listening to his wife, but also watching the television. At best he is only half-listening. Half-listening is not good enough. He will not understand what his wife was communicating with him. It is important to turn off the television or put down the newspaper, and give your spouse undivided attention.

It is important to take the time to listen to your spouse; you will value your spouse in doing so. What is she saying to you? Make sure you give good eye contact. It is important to inject the proper responses, making sure that you practically understand what she is saying. We can call these responses, "check points". This is important, because what one person speaks and what another person

Communication

hears, can be two different things. A check point may be, "If I understand you correctly, this is what you have said." When someone is sharing their story, it is like a path that has a beginning and an end. If you were hiking on a path through the forest, there will be check markers along the way, letting you know that you are on the right course. As a person is sharing their thoughts and stories, think of it as being a path where the conversation has a beginning and end. Be patient to hear the whole story, but offer comments to ensure that you understand her thoughts throughout her sharing.

We must remember that if our spouse is sharing with us, it must be important to her. If it is important to our spouse, then it should be important to us. Take it as a privilege that your spouse loves and thinks so highly of you that she wants to share these things with you.

Once we have taken the time to listen and understand what our spouse has said, we now have the right to speak. Let us remember that the thing that our spouse has valued is that we listened. Listening communicates love and importance. Your spouse may not even want you to say anything; the main thing is that you listened. Your listening will speak much louder than your words.

The words you speak will convey a lot too. As you respond, notice your tone of voice. Your tone of voice should communicate love, concern, empathy, warmth, and wisdom. When you speak, you are responding to what has been shared. Our words feed back into the context of our spouse's sharing. By doing this, we convey that we love our spouse and affirm her.

If we have not listened effectively, we will share a response that is irrelevant to what has just been said. This creates hurt. Our responses can be unloving and condescending when we haven't taken the time to listen properly.

The Apostle Paul wrote in 1 Corinthians 13:1, "If I speak in the tongues of men and of angels, but have not love, I am only a resounding gong or a clanging cymbal." It is so important that we communicate in love. When we listen and speak in love, this will build up our marriages.

STUDY QUESTIONS

1. Name someone who is a good communicator?
2. How have good communicators been a strength to you?
3. How does prayer influence your character? Your wisdom? And your attitude toward other people?
4. Give some examples of your nonverbal communication with your spouse?
5. What divides your attention when you communicate with your spouse?
6. It is important to speak in love. When are times when your speech has been hurtful?

3

MALE & FEMALE

"Wives, submit to your husbands as to the Lord. For the husband is the head of the wife as Christ is the head of the church, his body, of which he is the Savior. Now as the church submits to Christ, so also wives should submit to their husbands in everything." (Ephesians 5:22-24)

A key to a good marriage is understanding what it means to be male and female. I have had husbands say, "I don't understand my wife." The reason why they don't understand them is because they are females. They think that their wives think like they do. I have also had wives say, "I don't understand my husband." They have to understand that they are married to males who are very different from them. God has created males and females as equals, but very different. When couples learn the differences, this will strengthen their marriages. They will realize that the differences are not a threat, but rather, a beautiful compliment to each other.

We live in the antitheses of life and creation. This is where everything has an opposite. These opposites live in a balanced relationship with each other. Some examples of antitheses are: hot and cold, light and darkness, and male and female. Even though these are opposites, one will have a strength over the other. Hot will have strength over cold, light will have strength over darkness, and the male will have a strength over the female.

A husband's strength in marriage is not through being abusive or domineering, but rather in love. The Apostle Paul refers to the relationship that Jesus has with the church. It is a loving relationship. Jesus love will always be stronger toward the church, than the church's love for Jesus. The husband is to love his wife as Jesus loves the church. The wife is to love her husband as the church has love for Jesus.

The husband is to be the spiritual leader in the home. It is the husband who takes the initiative to lead the family in daily prayer and devotions. It is the husband who takes the leadership of bringing the family to the house of God for worship. When the father fails to be present with the family in worship, the likelihood that the children will continue in the church is small. When the father is present, setting an example for his children, the likelihood that they will continue in the church is very high.

Wives want their husbands to be leaders. When the husband sits on the couch being apathetic, and the wife has to do all the leading, she begins to resent it. The wife resents it when she is the one encouraging the children to get their homework done, and the husband takes no interest. The wife resents it when she is the one taking the children to church and teaching them Christian values, and the husband takes no responsibility.

Men are by nature independent. They like to be problem solvers, and resent people giving them advice. They may have one close friend they can confide in, but for the most part they keep their thoughts and feelings to themselves. Success is important to a man. They like status, position, and titles to define whom they are as successful and important. Men like to have control of their personal life, house, and work. Men like approval and praise.

Women by nature are more interdependent. They like to solve problems together. They are more social than men. They are more emotional than men. Women want to feel loved, secure, and validated.

Men are in conversation to find out what the problem is and then solve it. Women like to have conversation to be in relationship with others. It is common for a husband and a wife to come home from work, the husband sits down to read the newspaper or watch television, while his wife will begin to converse with him. He starts to feel annoyed, wondering what the point is. Once he thinks he knows what the point to her conversation is, he will then give her the solution to what he thinks is her problem. She resents this, because she doesn't have a problem, nor wants a solution. There may not be a point to her conversation other than wanting to be in relationship with her husband. When husbands realize that their wives are conversing to be in relationship with them, they will turn off the television or put down the newspaper, and take the time to nurture their relationships.

Wives need to relax in the car, while their husbands are trying to find the place where they are traveling. They will eventually figure it out, but to give them advice to stop and ask for directions takes away from their manhood. Wives be patient as you watch your husbands struggle to resolve hopefully what are small problems.

Societies over time may condition what it means to be a male and a female, but yet there are things that are innately different about them no matter what societies conditioning may be. Roles of males and females may change, but their being male and female do not. In the 1960s and 1970s, the role of the husband was to go to work and bring home the paycheck. The role of wives was to be the homemaker. The husband's role around the house was to take care of the lawn, the garage, and being the handyman. The wife was to take care of the inside of the home, cooking, laundry, dusting, vacuuming, and dishes. Now both men and women are working, so household roles may change for couples. Wives maybe doing many of the "masculine" roles, and husbands may be doing what have been traditionally, "feminine" roles. Even though roles change, husbands still want to be men, and wives want to be women.

There is truth to the saying, "Behind every successful man, there is a great woman." This means that a wife can be very successful in life. She may even earn more money than he does, but when she encourages her husband this will build him up. A man needs praise and encouragement from his wife. I knew a man who graduated number one both of his high school and college classes. When he graduated from college he was offered a very high paying job, but instead felt called into the ministry. When it was time to give his first sermon, he did a great job, but his wife criticized every part of it. My guess is that over time, this young, confident man would be an inch tall, because his wife was tearing him down, rather than building him up. Even if the sermon was not good, she could have been positive to say, "Good job, just getting up in front of the congregation was a big step, we will improve from here." A husband needs the praise of his wife.

A wife wants to be treated like a woman by her

husband. She wants to be loved, feel secure, and validated by her husband. I knew a woman who was the highest paid doctor in the hospital. She had all the respect of her colleagues, but when she came home, her husband belittled her. A lot of this had to do with his own low self-esteem; she made more money than he did. Even though she was very successful in the world, when she came home, she wanted to be treated like a woman.

A man initiates love in the relationship. As a husband loves his wife, she will blossom and bloom. She will respond to him with a vivacious love. When a husband fails to love his wife, she will become cold. I once had a man say, "My wife is so cold." As we visited, it didn't take long before I realized that he was the one who made her that way. As a husband loves his wife, this is a warmth that he brings her to life. When a man takes the time to love and care for his wife, she ignites. He will see a happy woman.

A lawn that gets nurtured by rain comes to life. When it doesn't receive rain, it will parch and die. So it is with a wife that is not nurtured in love by her husband. A husband who takes the time to show love for his wife and who takes the lead, will nurture a vibrant marriage. It is important for husbands to give hugs, bring flowers, give chocolates, take the time to listen, spend time with her, and say, "I love you". When he does this, his wife will respond with praise, support, and the encouragement that he longs for. My wife does not like to watch football, but when I nurture her in love, soon she is sitting by me, not because she likes football, but because she likes and wants to be with me.

Sexual intercourse is a beautiful part of marriage. If a man takes the time to have the intercourse of communication, the intercourse of nurturing, the intercourse of caring, and the intercourse of validating his wife, then sexual intercourse will have meaning for her. If a husband neglects all these other intercourses then she will feel used when it comes to sexual intercourse.

It is a strength to a married couple when they understand what it means to be male and female.

STUDY QUESTIONS

1. Antitheses are opposites, such as, hot and cold. Can you think of other antitheses? How do antitheses complement each other?
2. God created us male and female. How do males and females complement each other?
3. Do you recognize some of the differences of being male and female? What are some of these differences?
4. Do you agree that the husband is to be the leader of the family? If so, how is the husband to lead?
5. Do you agree with the statement, "Men are generally independent, while women are interdependent?

4

LOVE

The word love can be a broad term. I may say, "I love pizza", and with the same breath say, "I love my wife." What does that mean? What is the meaning of love?

C. S. Lewis wrote a book entitled, "The Four Loves", in which, he defines four types of love. Love may mean different things based on the type of love that we are defining. The first type of love is affectionate love, which is having a general compassion for all people. When Jesus said, "Love your neighbor as yourself," this is affectionate love. You have a general compassion for people, most of whom you don't know. You may not have anything in common with some people; you may even find yourself on the other side of the fence when it comes to a lot of issues. This is the love that breaks down all barriers to care for others, even if they are strangers or different. The story of the Good Samaritan, Luke 10, is an example of affectionate love. The Samaritan helped another person who was a stranger and on the other side of a prejudicial fence. This is the love of God, which allows us to reach outside of ourselves to show a general affection for all people, even if society has divided us by race, religion, status, age, and gender.

The second type of love is brotherly love. This is a love that we share with those whom we live life with. This is the love that is shared with members who belong to the same family, the same church, the same club, the same workplace, and/or the same community. This love shows a mutual caring and compassion with those you live life with on a daily basis.

The third type of love is romantic love. This is a love for the things we like. I may say, "I love to cross-country ski down a beautiful trail." "I love to canoe down a rushing river." "I love flowers." This love takes on a deeper meaning when it comes to a relationship with another person. When a man says to a woman, "I love you", he is saying, "I am attracted to you for many reasons." A man and a woman may be physically attracted to each other. A man may be attracted to a

Love

woman by the way she looks, but he may also be attracted to her interests, to her abilities in certain areas, to her disposition, to her character, to her beliefs, and to her values. When you get enough attractions, then you realize that this is a person you want to unite in marriage with as husband and wife.

The fourth type of love is sacrificial love. Sacrificial love is where you are willing to give of yourself as a servant to others. You put other people before yourself. It is a selfless love. When Jesus said, "There is no greater love than this, that a man lay down his life for his friends." (John 15:13) This is sacrificial love. Jesus is our friend, and he has shown us this love by dying on a cross for our sins.

When Jesus says, "If anyone would come after me, he must deny himself and take up his cross and follow me." (Mark 8:34) When people commit their lives to Jesus in this way, they have sacrificial love for him. This is the love of a Christian. It is abiding in the sacrificial love of Jesus where we may say like the Apostle Paul, "I have been crucified with Christ. It is no longer I who live, but Christ who lives within me." (Galatians 2:20) This is the deep love that is shown between husband and wife, which they sacrifice for each other. The question is not, "What can my spouse do for me?" But, rather, "What can I do for my spouse?" Our sacrificial love for spouse is such that we are willing to lay down our life for him or her.

Gary Chapman wrote the book, "The Five Love Languages." There are many ways that people show and experience love, but there are five primary ways or languages that love is shown. They are: quality time, acts of service, physical touch, gift giving, and words of affirmation.

Quality time is time spent together. It is during this time that a couple bonds as they spend time in conversation, and enjoying each other. Quality time doesn't mean expensive time. A couple who goes for a walk on a nice fall day or spends an evening at home playing a board game is having quality time, just as a couple who is taking a trip to a distant paradise.

There was a couple who purchased an old home out in the country. They liked the home because it had a porch on the east side of the house and a porch on the west side of the house. In the morning, as the day was starting, the couple would go out on the east porch as the sun was rising. They would spend time talking about the day ahead as they were drinking their coffee. As they concluded their time, they would pray, asking God to guide them in the day. At the end of the day, they would sit on the west porch as the sun was setting. It was there they would reflect on the day. They would conclude the day in prayer, giving thanks to God.

Love

Acts of service is doing things for each other. This is everything from mowing the lawn, doing the dishes, making the bed, and running errands for each other. When a spouse does an act of service for his wife, she will feel loved. I knew a woman who enjoyed doing crafts and selling them at shows. Her husband would spend his time at the band saw, making all the parts ready for her to assemble. She always felt loved by his service.

Physical touch is showing love to your spouse through hugs, holding hands, back rubs, and sexual intercourse. A man who worked a job that required hard labor always felt loved when his wife would rub his aching shoulder.

Gift giving is showing love through what you give. Gift giving is not judged by the expense of the gift. When someone receives a gift it is an expression of love from the other. When a woman receives flowers, chocolates, and jewelry, she feels loved by her husband.

I knew a couple who farmed. When the husband died, I ministered to his grieving widow. She told me the thing she missed the most, was when her husband was working in the fields, he would come into a house with a bouquet of wild flowers that he picked for her. The flowers were beautiful, but they also communicated so much love that her husband had for her. Christmas and birthdays are fun for those who express love in gift giving.

Words of affirmation are words that we speak that build each other up in love. These words are words of praise and encouragement. When we hear the words, "I love you," "Good job," and "You are special", they make us feel good.

As important as all five of these love languages are, there is one or two that are dominant for each person. A person will say, "I feel loved when this happens." It is important to know what your love language is, but it is also important to know what your spouse's love language is. This is a way that you will connect with your spouse in a powerful way. My personal love language is words of affirmation, while my wife's love language is acts of service. The mistake that gets made is when I praise my spouse, thinking that I'm communicating love, when what she needs me to do is mow the lawn. Because I feel loved when I am praised, I think that is how my wife is going to feel loved. In reality, when I mow the lawn and have the outside of the house and yard looking nice is when she feels loved. As I mow the lawn, she feels loved, and her response is praise for the good job I have done, so I feel loved.

"Love…It always protects, always trusts, always hopes, always perseveres." (1 Corinthians 13:7)

Love

STUDY QUESTIONS

1. C. S. Lewis defined four kinds of love. How do you experience love in these four definitions: affectionate, brotherly, romantic, and sacrificial?
2. Why is sacrificial love important in marriage?
3. Based on Gary Chapman's five love languages, how do you experience each one: quality time, words of affirmation, acts of service, physical touch, and gift giving? What love language is dominant for you? What love language is dominant for your spouse?
4. When do you feel loved?

5

THE VOW

During the wedding ceremony, the husband and wife exchange marriage vows. These are promises that are bound legally, but more importantly they are bound together in love. In marriage a covenant is made. A covenant is a relationship that two people have with each other. A covenant has a contract that is legally binding and there is a sign in the covenant.

God is a covenant maker. God initiates the covenant by saving his people. God gives a promise, a blessing, and a sign in the covenant. In return, God expects his people to respond in faithful obedience to him. God made many covenants with his people, but the greatest one that we celebrate as Christians is the covenant that God has established with us in Jesus Christ. God initiates the covenant by sending his son, Jesus, to save us. Through Jesus' death and resurrection, we have been set free from sin, death, and the power of the devil. We have been given forgiveness, rebirth, and the promise of eternal life. The sign of this covenant is the cross. The sign ever reminds us of the sacrifice that God made to save us, it reminds us of the forgiveness of sins and the promise of eternal life, and it also reminds us to live and walk by the Holy Spirit in our lives.

The Bible teaches us that Jesus is the bridegroom and we, the church, are the bride. I once was explaining this during a Sunday morning children's sermon, when one of the boys said, "Hey, wait a minute. A bride is a girl and I am a boy. A bride wears a dress and I don't wear dresses." As I looked out at the congregation and saw all the men, I asked, "How many of you are willing to be called the bride of Jesus?" They all raised their hands. I was wearing my clergy alb that looks like a dress, and said, "This dress represents the robe of righteousness that Jesus gives." I said, "The only time that we guys will be called a bride and wear a dress is when we are called the church." We must remember that we are living in a covenant of God's love and grace. God is the father and we are his children. Jesus is the bridegroom and we are the bride.

The Vow

Marriage is a covenant where promises are exchanged. The sign of the wedding covenant is the wedding rings. The rings are a circle representing eternity. A ring has no beginning and no end, so is the love that God has for us in sustaining marriage. The ring is also made of a valuable metal. The vows that we exchange, the life that we share, and God who binds us together is of the greatest value.

The marriage lasts when a husband and a wife are faithful to each other until death parts them. Their vows and promises are steadfast, now and forever. We have a relationship with God, because God is faithful. Faithful meaning, you can be counted on. God is the same yesterday, today, and tomorrow. God's love and promise toward us is never changing. How would it be if God was changing, one day he loved us and the next day he didn't? It would be hard to have a relationship with him. God is consistent; we can put our faith in him.

"The grass withers and the flowers fall, but the word of our God stands forever." (Isaiah 40:8) Everything in this world is subject to change, decay, and death. Everything about God is about consistency, life, and resurrection. Everything in this life is temporal, while everything about God is eternal. There is one thing that is a constant for us, and that is the word of God. The word of God does what it intends. When God speaks his word, creation comes to be. God sends his living word, who is Jesus Christ, God in human flesh.

"As the rain and the snow come down from heaven and do not return to it without watering the earth and making it bud and flourish, so that it yields seed for the sower and bread for the eater, so is my word that goes out from my mouth: It will not return to me empty, but will accomplish what I desire and achieve the purpose for which I sent it." (Isaiah 55:10-11) God will accomplish what he intends through his word. Just as the rain will water the earth bringing it to life, so will the word of Jesus bring us to life through his death and resurrection. In Jesus, our sins are forgiven, and we are given the promise of eternal life. God has given to us the resurrection life of Jesus in the Holy Spirit who is the guarantee of our salvation. Living in relationship to the Holy Spirit gives depth to our personal word and the promises we make.

In the marriage vow, you are making a promise of your word. We make promises only if we are one hundred percent certain that we can keep them. Our whole person is wrapped up in the promise. When we break our promise, we break our person. The word of our person represents who we are: integrity, attitude, belief, values, and trust.

When I perform wedding ceremonies, the couple signs the marriage license afterwards, making it legally binding. Often when a couple signs their marriage license, there is someone who will say, "Now it is official!" It is not the license that makes marriage official, but rather, your word. Here is how official the marriage license is: the very next day, you can get a divorce. It is your word, that makes marriage official, without your word, the license means nothing.

As people live their lives in faith, there needs to be accountability. The question that couples need to ask is, "Who are you accountable to?" As people go to work, they know who they are accountable to. They are accountable to their supervisor. A student in school is accountable to his professor. When it comes to marriage, who are you accountable to? Some will say, "Self", while others will say, "My spouse." The problem with this is that people change, as the world changes. A person may be getting married today, because this is what is good for him or her; but in five years as the world changes, your spouse changes, and you change, marriage doesn't seem to be the best thing for you anymore. Your accountability to self will not help your marriage, nor your accountability to your spouse whom you don't want to be married to anymore. This is where in life, we are ultimately accountable to God. On that final day, we will have to give an account of the decisions that we make, and the life that we have lived. When a person lives their lives in God, they are living in a sea of God's love and grace. It is this sea that will nurture the promises and the vows that we make. Even though we, the world around us, and others change; God's love and grace will sustain us. God will help a married couple adapt to the changing times. Even though their reasons for being married are different many years later, their purpose for being married is as strong as it has ever been.

I knew a man, who, when he got married, had the strong conviction that this is what was best for him in life. He also saw himself as being accountable to himself and spouse, but not God. After 18 years of marriage, and now having three children, he decided one day to leave. He left his wife, children, and promise behind. He is now "sworn to fun and loyal to none." He is 42 biological years old, but has the maturity of a rebellious seventeen year old. If this man had seen himself as being accountable to God, he would have been maturing in the ways of God. God would have given him the loving desires for his wife and children, and also the wisdom and strength to adapt to his changing world. Because this man was accountable to self and not God, he was selfish and only considered his own needs, leaving his family to fend for themselves.

An important aspect of God's love in our marriage vow is commitment. Many couples co-habitate, rather than get married. Some do this because they have seen so many marriages fail, including their own parents. They do not believe in marriage, nor want to take the chance of going through the pain of a failed marriage. God has designed marriage to last a lifetime, and when we put our faith in God, marriage is fulfilling. When a couple does not get married, but rather are co-habitants, there is the attitude, "I'm going to be in this relationship as long as it is good for me, and once the other person is not serving my needs, it will be easier to part ways." A couple enters into the relationship out of a selfish attitude of getting something out of the person, while couples who get married are making a commitment to each other, and the attitude is not, "What do I get out of this relationship, but rather, what do I put into it?" The couple is not looking at each other's selfish needs, but rather putting the needs of their spouses first. A person who is committed in marriage is one who has the attitude of serving the other.

We must remember that partial commitment to anything, including relationships, do not work out. As God has given one hundred percent commitment to our relationships, we must do the same. By such a marriage commitment, we will live in the fullness of what God has purposed.

A couple's marriage vows will also show a passion for the purpose for which they have been called. Abraham and Sarah were blessed by God to be a blessing to others. This continues to be the Christian attitude of Christian couples. The blessing that we have received in Jesus is a blessing that we share with those around us. Many couples share their blessings by being connected to the ministry of the church. Various areas where couples can get involved are: worship, education, youth, service, and mission.

One of the most precious vows that we read in the Bible is the one that Ruth makes to her mother-in-law Naomi:

"But Ruth replied, 'Don't urge me to leave you or to turn back from you. Where you go I will go, and where you stay I will stay. Your people will be my people and your God my God. Where you die I will die, and where I will be buried. May the Lord deal with me, be it ever so severely, if anything but death separates you and me.'" (Ruth 1:16-17)

Ruth and Naomi's lives were filled with tragedy. Naomi's husband and two sons died. The one son had been married to Ruth. When Naomi wanted to return to her home country to be with her next of kin, Ruth wanted to go with her. Naomi discouraged her from coming because she had nothing more to offer Ruth. Ruth had so much love for Naomi that she could not live without her. She was bonded in a deep love. Ruth shared her vow with Naomi. As the story goes, Naomi's eventual next of kin was a man named Boaz, who had a large estate with many fields and workers. One day Ruth went into the fields to glean some of the produce when she caught Boaz's eye. Boaz fell in love with Ruth and they got married. They had a child whose name was Obed. Obed eventually had a son named Jesse. Jesse eventually had a son named David, who became the great king of Israel. It was to David's lineage that God promised the savior who was Jesus Christ. Ruth was a person of deep conviction. Her words and promises were ones that others could trust. God could trust Ruth and know that he could work his purposes through her life. Ruth and Boaz did not know what God's purpose for their marriage was when they got married. They trusted in God as they exchanged their vows. It was in their faithful obedience to God that the purposes of God were revealed to them. As a couple gets married, they exchange their vows of promise, knowing that God who is rich in grace and mercy will show them the purposes for which they have been called.

For each couple who puts their faith in Jesus, they will experience the blessedness of the savior Jesus Christ. God will enrich their lives with his eternal goodness day by day, until death parts them. Even though the world and life changes, and the years go by, God does show his steadfast love for us. God will supply all that a couple needs for each day; they will have reason to give thanks and rejoice.

I once visited a couple who was living in a nursing

home. As I visited with them in their elder state, the husband was frustrated. He said, "I know that we had our seventieth wedding anniversary, but the anniversary cards we received said, it was our sixty-eighth anniversary". I was trying to be helpful by asking, "What was the date of your wedding?" The man showing anguish on his face said, "I can't remember!" I asked his wife the same question, she too said, "I can't remember." I started to name years that would have been about this time, hoping that they would ring a bell, but not any of them triggered their memories. I thought, "There is beauty in this." Long since they have forgotten the date of their wedding, they are still married. Their vows, words, and promises, they made to each other are as alive and strong as they were the day they got married. It is one thing to be there for your spouse on your wedding day, and it is another to be there for your spouse in the end.

Think of your wedding promises as being like a penny that you throw off a ship into the ocean. You would never be able to retrieve it. So it is in marriage, as we make our vows before the Lord, it is like throwing them into the sea of God's love and grace. We will not be able to retrieve the vows, but that our word of promise continues to be nurtured and strengthened in the sea of God's love and grace.

STUDY QUESTIONS

1. Name some covenants that God made with people in the Bible. What are similarities of Biblical covenants and your marriage?
2. Marriage is designed to last a lifetime. God's word is eternal. What are ways that your marriage can be nurtured in God's word?
3. How is your wedding ring a reminder of the covenant you have made with God and your spouse?
4. Why is it important for your marriage to be legally bound? Why is your spiritual bond so important?
5. Who are you accountable to in life? Who is your spouse accountable to in life?
6. How is your marriage blessed by God? How is your marriage a blessing to others?

6

DREAMS AND GOALS

Mission statements define who we are and what we are about. I have been in factories, businesses, and companies where they have their mission statements placed throughout their buildings where workers can see them. The mission statement will give focus to all the workers. Even though the workers may be working in very different departments, they are all working for the common goal of the mission statement.

Churches have mission statements. The church that I am currently serving has the mission statement: "To Know Christ, And Make Christ Known." Everything the church does is either coming to know Christ or making Christ known to others. The mission statement is simple enough that everybody knows it, but yet broad enough to encompass many ministries. The mission statement keeps people focused in the same direction. They use their energies for this mission. If a church does not have a defined mission statement, then there is going to be much division as the church members will be polarized in their efforts. The mission statement is also a boundary; preventing the church to become something other than what God has intended for it to be.

Marriages are strong when couples have prayerfully considered what their mission statement is before God. Like a company or a church, it keeps the couple focused on a mutual mission. This gives the couple understanding of whose they are, and what they are to be about.

Joshua, who was a leader of God's people in Old Testament times, had a mission for his family, a mission that he was hoping that all of God's people would subscribe to. It is written in Joshua 24:15,

"But if serving the Lord seems undesirable to you, then choose for yourselves this day whom you will serve, whether the gods your forefathers served beyond the river, or the gods of the Amorites, in whose land you are living. But as for me and my household, we will serve the Lord."

Dreams and Goals

Just as Joshua was a defined leader, understanding his mission before God's people, so Joshua was a defined leader of his household, understanding his mission as a father.

A couple's mission statement will identify them, give them a calling and worth, and will give them a sense of purpose. An example of a couple's mission statement is: "We are children of God, called together as one for the causes of Christ." A couple that daily reminds themselves of their mission statement will be strong in unity. They know who they are and what they are about as they keep a focus in life and be able to deal with potential distractions. A lack of a mission statement will allow distractions of life to derail them.

When a couple has a mission statement for their marriage, they can establish goals for their marriage. With a mission statement, their goals have reason and purpose. A couple's goals will reflect their mission statement. They will not establish goals that contradict their mission statement.

It is written in Acts 2:17, "In the last days, God says, I will pour out my Spirit on all people. Your sons and daughters will prophesy, your young men will see visions, your old men will dream dreams."

There are steps to goal setting. The first step is getting

inspiration through prayer. The second step is having a dream or a vision that God gives you. The third step is establishing a goal based on the dream. The fourth step is finding the ways and means to accomplish the goal. The final step is seeing the goal become a reality.

I have an old paper coffee cup that I call my inspiration cup. I was at a conference listening to a speaker, when the Holy Spirit gave me the inspiration to write a book. It was a flow of inspiration. I was writing down the thoughts that were coming so fast. I was writing them on pieces of notebook paper and also the outside, of the coffee cup. I set the goal of writing the book, and then sending it to a publisher. I now have the reality of this inspiration in my book, "River Reflections."

I enjoy trains. I have a large model railroad set-up in my basement, and also have railroad memorabilia that I have collected over the years on display. One day I was in a train depot, when I noticed this picture of people cross-country skiing along the railroad tracks in the mountains. I thought, "Wouldn't this be a nice picture in my train room?" Not only do I like trains, I also enjoy cross-country skiing. I was making comments like, "What does a person have to do to get a picture like this?" The ticket master was not biting at my hints. He did share that the picture is an actual place out in western Montana. This was a dream that I shared with my wife when I got home.

Dreams and Goals

We could ride the train to this place where they let us off, and there are some of the nicest cross-country ski trails. I had recently gotten my wife cross-country skis and she took a liking to it. She said, "Let's go!" I was able to purchase a package deal, and two months after having the dream, we were cross-country skiing in the mountains of western Montana. It was a wonderful time to bond with my wife. That was the most precious reality of it. The inspiration and goal that I had was to ride the train and go cross-country skiing, God's inspiration for us was an opportunity to bond together.

Goals are important. When a couple has goals, they spend time together working hard to make them reality. As a couple establishes goals, they need to have a realistic time line for accomplishing them. Are there goals that can be accomplished in one year? Some goals may be more long-term. It is good to have some five year, ten year, and even twenty-five year goals. Once you have accomplished a goal, it is good to establish new ones, some stemming from those that have already been achieved. I know a man who went to college; his goal was to get a Bachelor of Science degree in physics. When he accomplished this goal, he went to a university where he got his masters degree in physics. After accomplishing that goal, he went to another university where he got his doctor of physics degree. After getting his doctorate he taught as a professor of physics at a university. This shows that either you have to accomplish your big goals over time in many stages; or as you accomplish one goal, that leads to others.

There are three types of goals that a couple may have. They are: survival goals, personal goals, and purpose goals. Survival goals are goals that we make for our basic needs. These needs are: food, shelter, clothes, heat in the home, income, and health care.

The second type of goal is personal. I set a goal of running the Boston Marathon. Through hard work, I was able to accomplish this goal. A couple may set the goals of buying a house, buying a vehicle, raising children, traveling, and having their careers going strong. When we accomplish these goals, there is personal satisfaction that helps us to gain confidence in life. Many couples never look beyond this type of goal. These goals are worldly in nature, and serve the self.

The third type of goal is purpose. These goals are the ones that are spiritual. These are goals that look outside of self to the needs of others. Couples set these kinds of goals when they ask, "What purpose does our marriage have outside of ourselves?" God blessed Abraham and Sarah to be a blessing to others. The great blessing that God gave to Abraham and Sarah that has been shared to all people of the world is the savior, Jesus Christ. A couple prayerfully asks how they can serve in the church, in the community, in the neighborhood, and in their extended family.

The Apostle Paul wrote in Philippians 3:14, "I press on toward the goal to win the prize for which God has called me heavenward in Christ Jesus." Paul's goal was the heavenly kingdom, and that is ultimately the goal that all Christians have in Jesus. Christian couples have their goal of the eternal kingdom; they nurture each other in the Holy Spirit. It is through this nurturing that couples become more Christ-like, and develop a passion for the purposes of Christ. The couple develops heavenly goals that serve the world they live in.

When working with couples in their pre-marriage counseling, many of the goals seem obvious: getting our careers established, buying a house, and raising a family. When couples reach their twenty-fifth year anniversary, what is their reason for staying married? I have known many couples who have struggled with goal-setting after twenty-five years when their house is paid for, their family raised, and their careers are doing well.

Following a worship service, as I was greeting the people at the back of the church's sanctuary, I noticed a dear elderly couple of the church. They were walking out together. He was leaning on her, and she was leaning on him. If it wasn't for them leaning on each other, individually neither one of them would have been able to walk out of the church. As I looked at this couple, who have been a great example of marriage, I thought, "This is what marriage is about, leaning on each other." As we lean, both husband and wife are leaning on Jesus, who is the bond of marriage. Jesus is like the keystone of the two leaning sides of an arch.

"Trust in the Lord with all your heart and lean not on your own understanding; in all your ways acknowledge him, and he will make your paths straight." (Proverbs 3:5-6)

As a married couple leans on Jesus, he gives to them the love and wisdom for each day. God will guide them in the paths of his purposes. The goals that God inspires a couple to pursue are always the most fulfilling.

Dreams and Goals

STUDY QUESTIONS

1. Mission statements define our purpose in life. What is your mission statement as a couple?
2. What are goals that reflect your mission statement? What are one year goals? What are three-five year goals? What is a ten year goal?
3. What are examples of the stages of dreams, goals, and reality in marriage?
4. What are your survival goals? What are your personal goals? What are your purpose goals?
5. Proverbs 3:5-6, refers to leaning on God. How do you see your marriage as being like two leaning arches on the keystone being God?

7

FINANCES

"The earth is the Lord's, and everything in it. The world, and all who live in it; for he founded it upon the seas and established it upon the waters." (Psalm 24:1-2).

God is the creator of the world, and we are the stewards of creation. The world is limited in space and in resources, but when managed properly, the world can produce enough for all the people of the world. The problem comes when there is injustice with the distribution of resources. I remember as a child one Easter morning, waking up to go on an Easter egg hunt, when one of my three brothers got up very early in the morning and found all the Easter eggs. My brother thought all the Easter eggs were his. Some people would argue that the Easter eggs were my brother's, after all he was the early bird to get the worm, and he did work hard to find them all. My parents took a percentage of my brother's eggs and distributed them to the rest of the brothers. My parents' reasoning was not about ambition, but rather, distribution. There were only so many Easter eggs and four boys. Like the Easter eggs, the world's resources are limited to all its inhabitants. If one person who is ambitious consumes more than his fair share of resources, this means that others will go without.

Marriage and finances have to do with what we value in life. What helps married couples is getting priorities right. It is important to seek God as being our highest value.

Jesus said, "Do not store up for yourselves treasures on earth, where moth and rust destroy and where thieves break in and steal. But store up for yourselves treasures in heaven, where moth and rust do not destroy, and where thieves do not break in and steal. For where your treasure is, there your heart will be also." (Matthew 6:19-21)

Everything of this world is subject to change, decay, and death. When we put our trust in temporal things, they do not last. God gives his eternal presence to us that we have life, freedom, and heaven. When we put our trust in God, we have his eternal values in heaven as well as on earth. If we could put together all the energy in the world, all the resources of the world, all the worldly knowledge, and all the money in the world; together they would not have the power to save us. Our salvation comes from outside of this world. It is a gift of God in Christ Jesus. The most precious values in life are the ones that come from God. God helps us to discern what is of value in life, and what is not.

Having a marriage based on Jesus gives us contentment. King David wrote in Psalm 23:1, "The Lord is my shepherd, I shall not want." When we have Jesus as our shepherd, our hearts are content. Our spirit's longing is satisfied. When we do not have spiritual contentment in Jesus Christ, then we are always in want. Our human nature is such that we will always want more, enough is never enough. This appetite is such that it can never be filled. We can gain the whole world and not be satisfied. Once again, the world cannot produce what will satisfy our inner longings; only God can do that. Jesus said, "I am the bread of life, he who comes to me will not hunger, and whoever believes in me will never thirst." (John 6:35) It is important for a married couple to be content in life. I know some couples who have so very little in this world, but yet are so happy. I know other couples that have everything, but are not happy. The issue has to do with contentment.

It is easy to fall into the trap of thinking that the world and all of its goods can make us happy. Not even our spouses can make us ultimately happy. When we are looking for external things to make us happy, we will be frustrated in life. The world cannot produce happiness for us. Happiness comes from within; it is the Holy Spirit dwelling in our hearts that makes us content.

A Christian couple's attitude is one of thankfulness. It is easy to complain about many things. We can complain about what we do not have. It is easy for us to look at the Jones and feel like disadvantaged people. It is important to not compare ourselves with others, but to give thanks for all of what we do have in life. People have so much to be thankful for. A thankful heart is the best antidote for complaining. The Apostle Paul writes in 1 Thessalonians 5:18, "Give thanks in all circumstances for this is God's will for you in Christ Jesus." There is enough that goes wrong in a day, so it is important to have a thankful attitude, this will help couples to recognize God's abundant love and goodness for every day. A good exercise is to write a list of all the things that you are thankful for. You will be surprised at how long the list will be. It will supersede your complaints. It is good to rejoice and give thanks for all of God's goodness.

A Christian couple will be generous. Our human nature has a desire to be greedy. A greedy person does not ask what he can give, but rather what he can get. An attitude of greed will destroy marriage, and when you have enough greedy attitudes, it becomes a strain on society. People with generous attitudes give to the needs of others, have a strong marriage, and build-up society.

A Christian couple's attitude toward giving begins with God. God has given to us creation, life, and the savior Jesus Christ. God has given to us 100% of all we have. We give back first fruits, a percentage of what he has first given us.

An elder of a church called on a young family encouraging them to support the ministry of their local church. The husband said, "We can't, we are having a hard time paying the bills the way it is." The elder asked, "Can you give 1%?" The husband figured out what 1% would be and said, "I spend more than that on cigarettes." He said, "I can give one percent." That man increased his giving by 1% every year, until many years later he was giving 12% of his income to the church. As he gave to God, God honored his faithfulness. When we give to God, God will honor that giving and provide even more. When we can be trusted with a little, soon God trusts us with more.

In the Christian tradition, we make it our aim to give 10%, or a tithe, as an offering to God. Some give more than 10%, while others give less. Many like the young husband will start by giving a percentage and then increase it by a percentage each year until they are able to give a tithe.

The prophet Malachi wrote, "Bring the whole tithe into the storehouse, that there may be food in my gates of heaven and pour out so much blessing that you will not have room enough for it. I will prevent pests from devouring your crops, and the vines in your fields will not cast their fruit." (Malachi 3:10-11)

God will bless the couple that tithes. 10 cents of every dollar goes to support the work of God. This doesn't mean that the couple will spend the other ninety cents frivolously, we must be good stewards of all the money that God has given to us, making sure that we always use it for God's glory. Tithing is a step of faith, and God promises to bless those who take this step.

Here are important lessons to live by:

1. Understand the difference between your needs verses your wants. Needs are the essential things for life. They are not optional. They would be such things as: Food, clothing, insurance, health care, and shelter. Wants are things that are not essential for life, but we would enjoy having them based on our interests and hobbies. We may want a boat, but we need food to eat. Unless you want to eat your boat, make sure your needs are met before you seek after your wants.

2. Live within your means. We must remember that contentment comes through having our inner-self satisfied in Jesus Christ. The world will try to convince us that we need everything to be happy. If we fall into that thinking, we will begin to spend beyond our income. It is important to deny ourselves of our many wants and say, "No". This will prevent a lot of stress on your marriage.

3. It is important to budget. A budget will help us no matter what our income is. An example of a budget would be as follows: 10% - Offering to the church; 36%-Home, 22%-Food, 16% Automobile, 5%-Insurance, 5%-Clothing, 4%-Entertainment, and 2%-Miscellaneous.

4. Try to keep debt to a minimum. There are certain things that you purchase by taking out loans, like a car or a house. Make sure that your mortgages can stay within the means of your budget. Avoid reckless spending, impulse spending, and credit card spending. We need to pray that God will give us self-control, and the wisdom not to do these things. When we use a credit card, the interest that we are paying is very high.

5. It is important to live simply. As a married couple, when you love each other, the joy is being together. Going for walks, watching the sunset, or sitting at home watching a movie together will be precious. With so many of these activities, you haven't even spent a dime. If you don't have love for each other, then you can go on a trip to a paradise destination and be miserable. Enjoy the simple things in life, they will not be a strain on your budget.

6. We are living in a society that stresses instant gratification. We want everything our parents spent a lifetime working for now. We want something, and we want it now! It is important to say, "I would like this, but I need to save for it." You can make it a goal to save up money and buy it latter. By delaying gratification, we allow our impulses to calm down and think about things. When we do this, we realize a lot of the things we want on impulse are not things that we really need or really want.

7. It is important to save for retirement. The younger you are when you start a retirement fund, the better off you will be. The reason for this has to do with compound interest. For example, if a person saves a little each month in a stock mutual fund, that money will compound over time, giving you money for retirement. If you wait until you are older to start, then you will have to invest that much more to accomplish the same gain. There are those who reach retirement age who want to continue to work. It is good if you can put yourself in a position where that is an option. Some people cannot afford to retire when they reach retirement age, and may not have the health to continue to work a steady job. It is prudent to save in a retirement plan.

8. Determine your lifestyle. It is important for both

husband and wife to desire the same lifestyle. It will be difficult if one wants to live extravagantly, while the other wants to live simply. Sometimes income will determine the lifestyle you live, and other times it is your lifestyle that will determine the type of career you will pursue.

9. Learn to want what you have. We think that one more thing will make us happy. That one more thing leads to filled up attics, basements, and storage sheds. Instead of going to the store to purchase more things, open up the storage shed and enjoy what you have.

10. Be generous people. Giving to others will give you a sense of purpose in life. There is happiness in giving of yourself for the sake of Jesus and others. Instead of seeing what we can get in a day, we should see what we can give in a day.

Money cannot buy you happiness, but it is realistic to earn enough to meet your basic needs, and pursue some of your dreams. Financial stress can cause marital problems. It doesn't hurt to consult a financial advisor who can give you wisdom when it comes to finances.

When God fills our lives with the Holy Spirit, we have wisdom to align our priorities, the love for simple things in life, the strength to say, "No" to the unnecessary splurges, have generous desires that take away greed, and a thankful attitude to prevent us from complaining.

STUDY QUESTIONS

1. What are your top five priorities in life? What is your highest value?
2. The world belongs to God, how are you a manager of creation?
3. If you give to the church, what percentage do you give?
4. Of the ten suggestions, which one do you need to work on the most?
5. What are your needs? What are your wants?

8

CONFLICT

I once was at a Pastors' conference where the speaker was sharing about how he had been married for thirty-five years, and never once did he and his wife have an argument or a fight. The pastor sitting next to me, leaned over to a fellow pastor and said, "That must be one dull marriage."

As Christian people, we try to avoid conflict. We don't go looking for trouble, but even when we are trying to live a peaceful life, conflict does come. The world around us will put stress on our relationships. This chapter will give you some tools that can help resolve conflict.

The best way to prevent conflict is the way you live your life. The Apostle Paul writes in Ephesians 4:32, "Be kind and compassionate to one another, forgiving each other, just as in Christ God forgave you." This is where you allow the presence of the risen Jesus, the Holy Spirit to dwell in your life. When you open your life to God in prayer, and study the Word of God, the Bible, you develop a Christ-like person or attitude. A person who is kind, compassionate, and willing to forgive is looking to the needs, concerns, and pains of others with great sensitivity. People who are self-centered, selfish, arrogant, and brash are those who will have conflicts in their relationships. They do not have sensitivity to those around them.

As Christians, we wrestle with our human nature, and we will until we enter into heaven. It is there we will not have to contend with sin anymore. In this world we do not live perfect lives, even when we have a Christ-like nature. We still find ourselves rubbing others the wrong way, even though it is not our intention.

When a couple does celebrate their fiftieth anniversary, that is miraculous. It is God's grace working in two imperfect people that allows for a strong marriage that stands the test of time. It is the grace of God working in the couple that gives them the attitude to work through the times of conflict. Even in our best efforts, conflicts will come. Sometimes they may not be intentional or even our own fault. The key in our marriage is not whether conflicts will come, because they will, but it is how we learn to resolve the conflicts that will make the difference.

As conflicts come, you need to learn the emotional level of yourself and your spouse. As people, we need to differentiate between our mind and our emotions. We have these two parts. We are people who have emotions, and we are also people who have the mind to think with. Often, our emotions can override our thinking. When we get emotionally bottled up, we say things and do things that we will regret. It is hard to think straight when we are intoxicated with anger. When we think, we can figure things out. It is important to take care of our emotions, then we will be in the proper frame of mind to think.

When you feel your emotions bottling up like a fizzed up pop can, you need to call a timeout. It is good to develop a plan, so when you are in the heat of conflict, you can have an emotional awareness to call the timeout. You recognize that when the emotional state gets to a certain level, nothing productive will happen. Instead, things are only going to get worse. When a basketball team starts to play out-of-control, the coach has the awareness to call a timeout. This allows the team to calm down and regroup. That is what you are doing is calling a timeout to allow your emotions to calm down and then regroup.

When you call a timeout, you agree to be apart for a

time. This is a time when you take care of yourself. You need to de-escalate your emotions, and once you have done that you will be in a proper frame of mind to think things through. Healthy ways to take care of your emotions are to pray, go for a walk, lift weights, listen to peaceful music, and chop wood. When you pray, you allow the Holy Spirit to enter into your heart and mind. The Holy Spirit drives out the toxic emotions that fill our lives, and replaces those emotions with love and kindness.

When you come back after the timeout, you are in the frame of mind to think things through. The first thing that you do is define the problem. It is easy to try to treat the symptoms, but you need to find the rudiment that causes all the symptoms. The rudiment is the underlying issue that needs to be defined. Once you identify the issue, then you need to explore the options in resolving the issue that is creating the conflict. List all the options of resolving the conflict and then choose the best option. Once you have agreed on the best option to resolve the conflict, then explore the best resources for using that option. This is one method of resolving conflict.

Communication is very important for preventing conflicts and also resolving them. Sometimes what one person speaks and another person hears can be two different things. A husband can say one thing to his wife, and what she has heard is another. He doesn't know what he said has hurt his wife. This sometimes has to do with previous hurts, and so she may be presumptuous in her hearing. How does she respond to her hurt? One way is by blowing up in his face, and he is now hurt because she took the statement the wrong way and is not open to hearing him out or he is shell shocked to where he starts arguing back.

This leads to stonewalling, when neither the husband nor the wife will speak to each other. They are both hurt, but each feels that it is the other who owes an apology. A "hardness" sets in and the two start growing distant. The stonewalling can go on for some time. The longer the silent treatment continues, the harder it will be for them to resolve their differences. It is important for one of them to have the mature humility to break the ice. When you feel like your spouse needs to apologize, be mature, and also do an honest examination of yourself. Ask yourself the question, "How much am I to blame in this situation?" A lot of times we go by the premise, "I'm 100% right and my spouse is 100% wrong." If this is the case, ask yourself the question, "Could I be 5% wrong in the situation?" When you are honest, you will realize that the percentage is much higher to say, "I was wrong, we need to talk about it."

Another way that she can respond to the statement is through passive/aggressive behavior. This is when she does not want to have conflict. She overlooks the statement, but stuffs it in. Then as time goes by, another statement is made, and once again she stuffs it in. Eventually a statement will be made, and she blows up. He is wondering, "What has warranted this response?" It wasn't just that one statement, but the cumulative effect over time. The statement was the straw that broke the camel's back. The passive/aggressive response can also be subtle nitpicking or being critical toward him.

A good way to prevent and/or resolve communication conflict is through active listening. This is where you repeat almost verbatim what your spouse has said. "If I have heard you correctly, this is what you have said?" Your spouse can say, "Yes, that is what I said." Or, "No, that is not what I said." It will give a chance to clarify. If the husband says something that is hurtful, the wife can respond by saying, "If I heard you correctly this is what you said." He can say, "No", or "That is what I said, but it is not what I meant." It will allow him to make a disclaimer and then clarify. He could say, "That is what I said." What then does she say to try and resolve the hurt and prevent conflict? At this point, you make "I" statements rather than, "You" statements. "You" statements are accusatory. When someone says, "You", the other person will make a wall of defense. When this happens, there will be conflict. An "I" statement means

Conflict

that you have taken ownership of your hurt. You start the statement of saying, "I", then you name your feeling, and then you name the consequence because of what was said. You say, "I wonder why this was said, because now I feel sad, and I will never try that again." When you make this kind of a statement, your spouse will recognize the hurt and be compassionate toward you. Your spouse will now be empathetic to want to work through the hurt. He will ally with you rather than be your enemy. Your spouse does not want to hurt you and bring you down, or even if that was the original intent, once doing that, he will realize that was the wrong thing to do.

Perception can cause conflict. Each one of us has a perception screen. A perception screen is how we see something. Two people can witness the same event, but yet have different perceptions of what they saw. In these times it is important to ask each other, how did you see it? Take the time to listen, and try to see what your spouse sees. They may have perceived a different picture. When we understand the picture that they have seen, then it is easier to not take things personally, but rather for what they are. As a couple communicates their perceptions, soon they will be seeing the same picture and be able to resolve their differences.

When in conflict, it can be helpful to do a pros and cons list. You take the sides of the issue, and then you

The Tie That Binds

write out what the pros of choosing one option would be, as well as writing down the cons. By doing this, you can weigh out what would be the right option. I think of a couple who both had careers in the community they were living in. The husband had a successful medical practice, and the wife had a good position with a local company. The wife got a very good promotion, it would be her dream job. The problem was that they would have to relocate to another city. She wanted this job, while he couldn't leave his practice. They did have children and other things that would factor into making their decision. They made the pros and cons list for staying and also leaving. They factored in all the pluses and minuses of making their decision. What seemed like an impossible decision to make became an obvious one to them as they looked at the pros and cons.

Compromises are a good way to work through some conflicts. This is where you take your differences and try to find a workable happy medium. Nobody is going to be completely happy with a compromise, but yet it can work in resolving a conflict. If there is only one piece of pie left in the refrigerator and both want it, the compromise could be cutting the piece in half. I knew a couple who were taking the husband's parents out for dinner. As he was coming to the "T" intersection, he had to make a decision to turn left or right. There was a restaurant to the left and another restaurant to the right. As he was slowing down the car to make the stop at the intersection he asked, "Where do you want to eat?" His wife wanted to go to the restaurant to the right, while his mother wanted to go to the restaurant on the left. The husband didn't want to make either his wife or mother mad at him, so he said, "What is the compromise?" His wife said, "I'm paying for the meal, so let's go to the restaurant on the right." Sometimes it is good to create situations to work through, so you can practice working on compromises.

Direct confrontation is always the best when it comes to resolving conflict. If you have an issue with your spouse, go directly to your spouse. It is tempting to talk to a third person about your issue. This is called, "Triangling". You share your concern with this person, who then goes to the person you are having a conflict with. The problem is the third person cannot speak for you beyond the statement. The person you are having a conflict with will have all kinds of questions that the third person cannot answer. For that person now to go to you with these questions will just exacerbate the situation. Normally, the third person is the one who gets hurt in the process. Both people are mad at him, because he wasn't able to do what was expected of him in resolving the conflict.

A third person can be helpful in resolving conflict

when it is a friend who goes with you giving you moral support and encouragement. A third person can be helpful in resolving conflict when it is a trained professional counselor who can listen to both husband and wife, detect the problem areas, and then give prudent advice as to how to resolve the conflict.

Forgiveness is very important for resolving conflict, because it clears the air and puts the problem behind you. If a couple is at a healthy level in their relationship and a conflict arises, this will put them at a level that maybe unhealthy. When they are able to forgive, that puts them back at a healthy level. If they do not work through the conflict and they do not forgive, then they stay at an unhealthy level. When the next problem comes, then the level becomes worse, and eventually they are at a level that can be hard if impossible to resolve. Forgiveness will keep a couple's relationship at a healthy level.

The Apostle Paul wrote in Ephesians 4:26-27, "In your anger do not sin. Do not let the sun go down while you are still angry, and do not give the devil a foothold." I knew a couple who said, "The pastor who married us told us to 'Not let the sun go down on your anger'. We had many late nights working through our differences, but we always kept that principle for marriage." A marriage is healthy when a couple can resolve its differences.

Conflict

STUDY QUESTIONS

1. What are some conflicts that have come up in your marriage?
2. What are healthy ways that you relieve emotions?
3. As you think of recent conflicts, can you identify the issues? Explore options to resolve the conflicts. What resources are available in working the best option?
4. How do maturity and humility help to resolve conflict?
5. How will active listening prevent future conflicts in your marriage?
6. In working through conflicts, do you see the importance of "I" statements, rather than "You" statements?

9

TEMPTATION

I was a senior in high school, and it was the Friday morning of our homecoming football game. When I got to school, there was a buzz throughout the hallways. In the night, some of the opposing team players burned their school's initials into our football field. They were making claim to what belonged to us. That night, we defeated that team, and we reclaimed what was ours.

We are like that field. There is a spiritual battle that is waging in our lives. It is a battle between God and Satan. Satan wants to make claim to what belongs to God. God wants us to have a special life and marriage, while Satan wants to destroy our lives. Satan works subtly and craftily to drive wedges between couples and break down their marriages.

The Apostle Paul instructs us to put on the full armor of God:

"Finally, be strong in the Lord and in his mighty power. Put on the full armor of God so that you can take your stand against the devil's schemes. For our struggle is not against flesh and blood, but against the rulers, against the authorities, against the powers of this dark world and against the spiritual forces of evil in the heavenly realms. Therefore put on the full armor of God, so that when the day of evil comes, you may be able to stand your ground, and after you have done everything to stand. Stand firm then, with the belt of truth buckled around your waist, with the breastplate of righteousness in place, and with your feet fitted with the readiness that comes from the gospel of peace. In addition to all this, take up the shield of faith, with which you can extinguish all the flaming arrows of the evil one. Take the helmet of salvation and the sword of the Spirit, which is the word of God. And pray in the Spirit on all occasions with all kinds of prayers and requests. With this in mind, be alert and always keep on praying for all the saints." (Ephesians 6:10-18)

Like an athletic competition, there is offense and

defense used against the opposition. A couple's offense is working on your marriage daily in prayer, using good communication, expressing love, setting good goals, and being faithful to each other.

A couple also needs a good defense. God has given to couples the Sixth Commandment, "You shall not commit adultery." This commandment is to be exercised in love. When we love our spouse, then there is no thought of committing adultery. Although God's love for us is steadfast and never failing, our human love has its ups and downs. When our love wanes, the Sixth Commandment is a safeguard or a boundary that keeps us from committing adultery with someone else. This commandment is also exercised in love by supporting other couples' marriages. A Christian's desire is not to tear down another couple's marriage, but always in love to help build up their marriage.

When working with couples in their pre-marriage counseling, I tell them that the divorce rate is fifty percent. I ask the question, "Is there anything that your spouse could do that would end your marriage? If this were to happen, you couldn't stick with him or her any longer." The number one answer is: Infidelity. Most couples tell me, if their spouse were to be unfaithful, they would not be able to stay in the marriage. Jesus taught us that divorce is a sin, with the exception of adultery.

Jesus said, "It has been said, 'Anyone who divorces his wife must give her a certificate of divorce.' But I tell you that anyone who divorces his wife, except for marital unfaithfulness, causes her to become an adulteress, and anyone who marries the divorced woman commits adultery." (Matthew 5:31-32)

Adultery starts with a look of lust. If a person doesn't renounce that look, but entertains it by nurturing it with thoughts, this often leads to committing the act of adultery. It is important to take care of the lustful thought at its root. Jesus taught, "You have heard that it was said, 'Do not commit adultery.' But I tell you that anyone who looks at a woman lustfully has already committed adultery with her in his heart." (Matthew 5:27-28) Sin is a matter of the heart. Christians need to confess their sins daily, putting lustful desires to death by crucifying them with Christ. It is in receiving forgiveness and the Holy Spirit that God renews our hearts daily. Adultery is like a weed. It has its roots, its stem, and its fruit. When weeding a garden, the roots of the weeds lie underneath the soil, and we cannot see them. The stem provides the nutrients to produce the fruit, and the fruit of a weed is poisonous. Lust leads to the poisonous fruit of adultery. Jesus teaches us to uproot the lustful roots hidden in the heart through confession and forgiveness; we do not want to reap the fruit of adultery. Replace the lustful desires with the love of God who gives us self-control in temptation.

Even though a couple is married, they continue to live life with those of the opposite sex as they are part of organizations, work, and live in the community. Often couples will spend more time at the work place, working with coworkers of the opposite sex, than they do with their own spouses. Some of these people will be attractive, pleasant, helpful, and share common interests. It is very important to keep good working relationships with such people of the opposite sex while keeping professional boundaries.

I knew a Christian man who brought his family to worship every Sunday. He was faithful in instructing his children in the ways of the Lord. He served on various committees and boards in the church. He was a respected man as he had the top position in his work place, and he served on various boards in the community. In his weak moment, he crossed the line and committed adultery with a subordinate worker. This action cost him his position, his marriage, his family, his community, and his church. His actions were costly ones. It wasn't worth it.

Jesus teaches against divorce, calling divorce sin with the exception of adultery. I would also say that abuse fits into this category. It is not God's desire for us to live in an abusive relationship. When a woman is being abused by her husband, she needs to leave the environment. It takes a woman leaving her husband on average seven times before she leaves him for good. It is hard for her to leave because of all the personal investments that she has with him. Even though her husband abuses her, she still loves him. She sees good qualities in him that are often overshadowed by the abuse. She has high moral standards against divorce and doesn't want to feel like a failure in the marriage. She has children with her husband and is afraid of what adverse effect it may have on them. Her husband is often a good financial provider. I remember a woman who was being abused by her husband but wouldn't leave because her mother left her abusive father, only to have the family struggle financially. She was willing to take the abuse for the sake of her children having food on the table and shoes on their feet.

There is also alcohol abuse. In my ministry of working with struggling couples, the highest percentage has to do with alcohol abuse. I would have to say that alcohol abuse is the number one cause of divorce. An alcoholic is married to the bottle. It takes priority over spouse, over children, over money, and over time.

Gambling addiction is another abuse that has caused couples to divorce. Gambling is one of the most addictive things a person can get into. I knew a wife who gambled all of her husband's life savings away. I have known

Temptation

people to have gambled away their paychecks, and in some cases all of their life assets, including homes and farms. I have also known people who have embezzled tens of thousands of dollars from their work places to support their gambling addiction.

There are treatment programs and support groups that can help people who are struggling with addictions. The resurrection power of God has brought freedom to many people who are now recovering from their addictions.

Temptation comes to all couples. The best way to prevent the fall of temptation is putting on the whole armor of God. Daily, couples need to discipline themselves in prayer, in Bible reading, in worship, in fellowship with other Christians who share the same values, in Christian character, and in obedience to God's commandments of love.

When we fall to temptation, it is important not to give up, but to remember the words of the Apostle Paul, "Therefore, if anyone is in Christ, he is a new creation; the old has gone, the new has come!" (2 Corinthians 5:17) In Christ there is always a new day, we can be forgiven of yesterday's sins, and we can live with the confidence of the Holy Spirit as we go forward. God does not want couples to have the sins and guilt of the past to weigh them down in the future. Couples always need to be looking to the future, focusing on the love of Jesus, rather than looking backwards at the things that have troubled their past. If we walk backwards in life, we will trip and fall. Nobody can carry the burdens of the past and have a healthy outlook for the future. There are steps that Christian couples can follow to have a healthy outlook.

The first step is to admit sin and guilt. This is a hard step to take, but a necessary one. If we don't admit our sin and guilt, then we will continue to lie, deny, and make excuses for our wrongful behavior that will only perpetuate the problem. "If we claim to be without sin, we deceive ourselves and the truth is not in us. If we confess our sins, he is faithful and just and will forgive us our sins and purify us from all unrighteousness." (1 John 1:8-9) It is in confessing our sins, that we receive the promise of forgiveness. Jesus died on the cross and is risen from the dead, that we may cast all our sins and cares on him, knowing that he forgives us and loves us. As we examine ourselves of our sins and shortcomings, it is also important to acknowledge our good points as well. God works to redeem us, because we have many good qualities about our person. It is with these good qualities that God is able to rebuild our lives.

It is also important to ask forgiveness from those whom we have hurt because of our abusive behavior. As we receive forgiveness from these people and make amends with them, this also brings healing to our person.

Temptation

The second step is to receive the Holy Spirit. The Holy Spirit is the risen Jesus who now dwells in you. It is the Holy Spirit who gives you the power to be God's person. Jesus said, "Receive the Holy Spirit." (John 20:22) The Apostle Paul writes, "Don't you know that you yourselves are God's temple and that God's Spirit lives in you?" (1 Corinthians 3:16) It is the Holy Spirit dwelling in you, that makes you a new person of God. It is the Holy Spirit who gives you the power to overcome destructive behaviors. John writes, "You dear children, are from God and have overcome them, because the one who is in you is greater than the one who is in the world." (1 John 4:4)

The third step is to exercise spiritual discipline. Just as we brush our teeth daily to prevent tooth decay, so we exercise spiritual discipline to prevent us from living in the old sinful patterns that bring destruction. Three disciplines that give us spiritual strength are prayer, fasting, and service to others. Prayer is allowing the Holy Spirit to enter into our lives. Fasting helps us be dependent on God and not worldly things for our strength. Service to others helps us live a purpose beyond ourselves.

The fourth step is to have good goals. When we have goals established according to God's will for our lives, we stay focused. It is easier to say, "No", to the devil and temptation when we know what we are about in life. As

Christians, we keep our focus on God, and what he has purposed for our marriages.

The fifth step is to surround yourselves with people who are going to build you up and not tear you down. They share the same values that you do, and often share the same goals. They will provide support and encouragement to live the Christian life. If we surround ourselves with people who are into destructive behavior, it won't take long for us to fall into the temptations of what our friends are doing. When we surround ourselves with people who have a sincere faith in God, who delight in walking in the Holy Spirit, and want to glorify God in their lives; it will be much easier to say, "No" to the destructive desires that tempt us, and to say, "Yes" to the life giving purposes of God.

The sixth step is keeping the spark of love in your marriage burning within. This means spending time with each other, saving energy for each other, fostering romance, and share in your deepest emotional love. The Apostle Paul shares words of wisdom, "The husband should fulfill his marital duty to his wife, and likewise the wife to her husband. Do not deprive each other except by mutual consent and for a time, so that you may devote yourselves to prayer. Then come together again so that Satan will not tempt you because of your lack of self-control." (1Corinthians 7:3,5)

God is working to give us a spiritual mindset that is positive and confident. We can be like the Psalmist, "This is the day the Lord has made; let us rejoice and be glad in it." (Psalm 118:24) This mind set is a healthy one for married couples to have for each day of their lives.

STUDY QUESTIONS

1. How do you understand the sixth commandment as being a defense for marriage? How do you understand the sixth commandment as an "offense" of God's love for marriage?
2. As a married couple, what are the healthy boundaries you set with others in maintaining professional and friendly relationships?
3. What spiritual disciplines will you use to eradicate the roots of temptation?
4. What addictions, behaviors, and practices are most threatening to your marriage?
5. How do you plan on practicing the steps to freedom?

10

CHILDREN

Jesus loves children. One day as Jesus was teaching in a synagogue, mothers brought their children to him for a blessing, but the disciples rebuked them. This is when Jesus said, "Let the little children come to me, and do not hinder them, for the kingdom of heaven belongs to such as these." (Matthew 19:14) When the teacher taught in the synagogue, it was to be as quiet as a library. The teaching in the synagogue was for adults, and they did not want children to be a disruption. These mothers wanted their children to be blessed and to be in the presence of Jesus, even if it was at the risk of getting into trouble. Parents must be willing to do whatever it takes to bring their children into the presence of Jesus. Jesus' blessings are the greatest that children will ever receive. Jesus is the one who helps children to grow and mature in the ways of God.

When God created our first parents, Adam and Eve, these are the words that God gave to them, "Be fruitful and increase in number; fill the earth and subdue it." (Genesis 1:28)

Adam and Eve had two sons named Cain and Abel. Abel was one who herded animals, while Cain tilled the soil. As Cain and Abel made their offerings to God, God was pleased with Abel's offering, while he was displeased with Cain's offering. Abel gave his offering out of love and reverence to God. Cain gave his offering to God out of obligation. Abel gave first fruits offering to God, while Cain gave what little he had left for God. Children may have sibling rivalry, caused by jealousy. When God was pleased with Abel's offering, this made Cain jealous of his brother. Jealousy motivated Cain to kill his brother Abel. His blood was crying out from the soil that he tilled. When God confronted Cain, Cain's response was, "Am I my brother's keeper?" (Genesis 4:9) As Christians, the answer to that question is, "Yes". In love we are to love our brother and take care of his needs.

Cain represents humanity that has fallen away from God. Humanity does not show a loving devotion to God.

Children

Humanity's nature is sinful. People will try to have a relationship based on obligation, rather than love. What God wants is our loving heart's devotion to him. Abel represents Jesus, who is the righteous one before God. Jesus loved God and is our brother's keeper. Jesus showed his love for us by dying on a cross. Jesus was crucified because of humanity's sins, but it is by his blood that we are forgiven and saved. Jesus is the first fruits of those who have died (I Corinthians 15:20). We want to raise our children by Jesus' loving example.

As Christian couples, you honor Christ in your marriages. All that you do glorifies God. This begins with your worship of the Lord your God. Your worship life spills over into your everyday life. The Christian values that you have on Sunday morning are the values that you live throughout the rest of the week.

Joshua, a leader of God's people, was also setting the example to them of worshiping and serving the Lord.

Joshua said, "Now fear the lord and serve him with all faithfulness. Throw away the gods your forefathers worshiped beyond the river and in Egypt, and serve the Lord. But if serving the Lord seems undesirable to you, then choose for yourselves this day whom you will serve, whether the gods your forefathers served beyond the River, or the gods of the Amorites, in whose land you are living. But as for me and my household, we will serve the

Lord." (Joshua 24:14-15)

Joshua could not make the people worship and serve God, but he was making a proclamation to the people that he and his house will worship and serve the Lord. He was being an example for the people to follow. As Christian couples, we make the commitment to honor God and attend his house of worship, but also to open the door of our home, so that it too will be a place where we honor him. It is God whom we worship and dedicate our lives. We live by God's moral principles in life. We will establish a loving, secure, and stable Christian environment to raise children.

In Christian parenting, it is important to have daily devotions and prayer with children. This can be done during specific times of the day; morning, meal-times, and bed-time are good times. It is during these times that we have devotions of reading the Bible, prayer, and talking about spiritual topics with our children. We open our house to the Lord, and everyone is nurtured in the love of God. It is in this instruction that we encourage each other.

It is important to be engaged in the Holy Spirit every day; this keeps our focus on God. Because of our human nature, it doesn't take long to revert to having a worldly focus.

"Hear, O Israel: The Lord our God, the Lord is one.

Children

Love the Lord your God with all your heart and with all your soul and with all your strength. These commandments that I give you today are to be upon your hearts. Impress them on your children. Talk about them when you sit at home and when you walk along the road, when you lie down and when you get up. Tie them as symbols on your hands and bind them on your foreheads. Write them on the doorframes of your houses and on your gates." (Deuteronomy 6:4-9)

As humans, because we are by nature sinful, we suffer from a spiritual attention deficit. It doesn't take long to forget God's ways for our lives. We are to daily confess our faith in God. We are to love the Lord, and to show that love to our neighbors. God's people would write God's commandments on their doorposts, on their bracelets, and on their frontlets. They would also talk about the ways of God in their waking, at meal-times, and at bedtime. The Apostle Paul wrote, "Be joyful always: pray continually: give thanks in all circumstances, for this is God's will for you in Christ Jesus." (1 Thessalonians 5:16-18)

When parents establish a Christian environment for their children, they will have the peace of knowing they are being nurtured by their parents who love and care for them. They will also have a consistent understanding of what is right and wrong, and will grow-up with a respectful attitude toward God and others. They will know what is expected of them, as they learn the loving moral values that God has for them. When children are being raised without a moral understanding or conflicting value systems, they get confused. Rather than being defined as who they are as a person of God, they will conform to the values of those around them. Because they are living in a pluralistic society, they may develop a learned helplessness that leads to a rebellious attitude.

There are parents who use a very restrictive approach to raising their children. They give them no freedom to learn and grow in their environment, while other parents may have a permissive approach to raising children, where children are given no moral guidance. The Christian approach to raising children is balanced. They give their children the ability to explore and develop their own personal interests in life, but have established healthy boundaries in allowing this. Christian parents are always concerned about having children mature in God's love and grace, while encouraging their individuality before God to develop.

One of God's purposes in marriage is procreation, as mentioned earlier in the verse from Genesis 1:28. Some couples choose not to have children; there is nothing wrong with this choice. Other couples cannot have children because of medical reasons, and many couples have children through adoption.

For couples who are entering marriage, it is important to plan. There are many circumstances that will help a couple determine how many children they will have. One of these circumstances is financial. Children have a lot of needs from the time they are born to the time they enter secondary education. It is important for couples to financially plan for their children's needs.

Another circumstance is time. If both husband and wife are working, they need to determine the time and energy they will have to nurture their children. What assistance will a couple need to raise children, such as a daycare, and also in maintaining their children's demanding schedules? As they plan their family, this will determine how many children they can realistically have.

There is the circumstance of how many children a couple can nurture while maintaining the health of their own marriage. Children need a lot of attention, and sometimes in their effort of nurturing them; couple's marriages can weaken because of a neglect for each other.

As we plan for children, we must remember that they are ultimately God's plan. Children belong to God, and parents are called to be the loving stewards to raise children in his ways. When the day comes for children to leave the nest, we have done our job when they are confident to take flight into the world. As hard as it is to let our children go, we do children no justice in trying to keep them dependent on us.

Whether a couple plans their pregnancy or not, we must remember that God has given a couple nine months to prepare. When the child is born, the couple has made all the preparations in receiving the baby into the world and their lives. This way couples cannot say to a child, "You were a mistake" or an "Oops child". To tell your children this can be devastating to them. We must remember that life begins in the mind of God. The prophet Jeremiah teaches us this, "The word of the Lord came to me, saying, 'Before I formed you in the womb I knew you, before you were born I set you apart; I appointed you as a prophet to the nations.'" (Jeremiah 1:4-5) We must understand that every child was first created in the mind of God, and that each child God has a special purpose for.

It is God's plan that sex is for couples who love each other and have committed their lives to each other in marriage. With this understanding, we also realize that many children are born outside of a marital relationship. We must believe that in God's love and mystery, each child was purposed by God, and each child is loved by God. I knew a family where there was a husband and wife who loved each other. This couple had six children. Not all of these children were of the same biological father.

Children

The mother told me, "The one son wants to be just like you Pastor Jeff." I took this as an honor. One day I had this boy out for supper, and I asked him, "Do you ever see your biological father?" He paused and said, "My mother was raped." At this point I felt my heart sink, but it gave me even more respect for the mother who gave this boy a chance at life. This boy, whom God loves, has been a blessing to his mother, to so many people, and to me. We are not to be concerned so much about how a person enters into this world, as we must remember that we are reborn as children of God through baptism and rebirth. It is in baptism that we are given a spiritual birth and we are claimed as God's child.

As Christian couples, if we are waiting for the perfect time to have children, we will never have them. If we feel that we are inadequate to raise children in this world, the world will tell us that we are. Couples of every generation are told, "How can you bring a child into this cruel world?" Couples need to put their faith in God, knowing that God will be with them to raise their children. When we put our confidence in God, we will be parents who raise children to make this world a better place. Don't let the Devil cast doubt about raising children who can experience the joy of living a Godly life. They will be difference makers. This is the bold and confident attitude that parents must have in each generation.

The Tie That Binds

My wife, Andrea, and I have two children. We had planned on having two and we are thankful to God for them. If we would have had three or four children, that would have been fine too. I remember when Andrea and I got married everything was great. When the time came that she was pregnant with our first child, the thought came to me, "Will this disrupt our wonderful relationship?" Our first child was born and I wouldn't have wanted life any other way. It was just perfect, the three of us. When Andrea was pregnant with our second child, I thought, "Will this disrupt this perfect relationship that the three of us have?" When our second child was born, I wouldn't have wanted it any other way. Life is now best with the four of us. I believe it is God's design that if we would have had more children, I wouldn't have wanted it any other way. Children are special gifts from God.

Again, it is important for couples to nurture their relationship when raising their children because they can subtly drift apart. It is common that a couple will get a divorce, because they have drifted apart. They look at each other and ask, "Who are you?" I knew a couple that went out every month on the date of their marriage. They went out on the 8th day of each month, as a discipline to nurture their marriage. If they didn't have this discipline, they would never have had the time to spend with each

Children

other.

When a child is born, it is important for parents to bond with him or her immediately. It is important to hold the child, read to the child, speak to the child, and pray with the child. So much of a child's personality is being formed in those first months of life. It is there that they will develop a trusting bond with you, that will also be healthy in bonding with others as they get older. As the child grows and matures, it is vital to keep a nurturing bond with your child.

As you bond with your children, you nurture their faith, and nurture their self-confidence. As children develop their personalities that will show a Christ-likeness, we also know that they develop interests in life. Even though children grow up with the same parents, live in the same house, go to the same school, and have attended the same church, they may each be very different people. Parents are not to have a "cookie cutter" approach to raising their children, but learn to understand each child as his own individual person. In a family you may have one child who is a good athlete and loves science. It is unfair for parents to have the same expectations for the next child. The next child may resent and rebel against parents and others who would have the same expectations for him. The next child may be more interested in music and studying history. Each child needs to excel in his own interests. Parents also have to guard against trying to fulfill their lifelong personal goals through their children. If a father had the hope of being a great athlete, it will be a disservice to his children to now live this dream vicariously through his children.

Children learn through association. As a child, I remember the symbol for poison was the skull and crossbones. That association prevented me from drinking or playing with substances that were harmful to me.

Another way that children learn is through the modeled behavior of others. That is why it is important for parents to be good role models, and to surround their children with other good role models. Children will learn from the example of others, whether it be good behavior or bad behavior. I tell parents that they will have the greatest influence on their children. Children emulate their behavior more than anyone else's.

Children learn through positive reinforcement and negative reinforcement. Positive reinforcement is when we reward good behavior, while negative reinforcement is giving consequences for bad behavior. Good communication helps with this process. When a child is told the reason why good behavior is important and the rewards that come with it, he/she will understand the context of good behavior for their lives. The same must be communicated about bad behavior. Children have a

Children

mind to think and reason with. They will learn from their intellect why some behavior is good and other behavior is bad.

Each parent must develop a way to discipline that will not kill the child's spirit, but will help train them in doing what is right. Working with children to develop a contract that is reasonable and fair is important when it comes to discipline, so when there is an infraction, the parents are not perceived as bad. They have transgressed the contract that they have helped design.

Consequences must fit the bad behavior. Some disciplines that have been effective are time-outs, withholding privileges, and occasional spankings. Time-outs should last a certain length of time. The rule for time-outs is one minute multiplied by the age of the child. If the child is five, then a five minute time-out is appropriate. Withholding privileges will often prevent children from engaging in bad behavior.

I discourage spanking. If parents spank their children, it should only be done for extremely serious things. A spanking should be on the buttocks. Hitting a child anywhere else is abusive. If a child runs out on a busy street, a spanking will help a child associate the pain that will prevent them from running into the street again. Parents who spank as their main way of disciplining their children run the high risk of destroying their confidence.

Children will establish their roles in the family. One child will be in the role of a leader, another child will be in the role as the comforter, another child will be in the role as the peacemaker, and another child will be in the role of the clown. These roles do not change as the family gets older. Even as adults, these children have the same roles. In ministering to families in crisis, I can always see the roles the children have taken. It is also interesting because the role that a child has in the family is also the role he or she will have in community and church. If a child's role is being the leader in the family, as adults they are often taking leadership roles in the church and community.

The Fourth Commandment is, "Honor your Father and Mother." It is important for children to honor their parents with respect and dignity. God has given parents as shepherds to love, protect, nurture, and provide for their children. The values' parents teach their children will be the values that they will live by and eventually pass to their children. This commandment is given with the assumption that parents are raising their children in the ways of God. The Apostle Paul wrote in Ephesians 6:1-4, "Children, obey your parents in the Lord, for this is right. 'Honor your father and mother'-which is the first commandment with a promise- 'that it may go well with you and that you may enjoy long life on the earth.' Fathers, do not exasperate your children; instead, bring

Children

them up in the training and instruction of the Lord."

Parenting is challenging. It has its rewards, and also its disappointments, especially when children rebel and get into trouble. This is where we must be vigilant in prayer, and love our children, helping them to get through a season of difficulty. Remember the wisdom of Proverbs 22:6, "Train a child in the way he should go, and when he is old he will not turn from it." No parent is perfect, we make mistakes, but we must remember that by God's grace, we can raise our children to have a spiritual foundation.

STUDY QUESTIONS

1. As Joshua dedicated his house to God, how do you honor God in your house?
2. What were ways that the Israelites reminded themselves of God's ways and instruction? Why was this important? What are ways that you will daily remind your children of God's instruction for life?
3. How will you instill God's moral values in your children?
4. Who will assist you in raising your children?
5. How will you maintain a strong marriage, as you nurture and raise your children?
6. How will you discipline your children?

11

STORMS

A certain lady would come to church every Sunday. After the worship service, she would meet with other people during the coffee hour. She enjoyed bragging about her daughter and family. Her daughter and son-in-law lived in a big house, drove luxurious cars, frolicked with recreational vehicles, and took many trips. This woman's daughter and son-in-law had very well paying jobs. There was an economic recession, and the couple lost their jobs. In time, they lost their home and possessions. The greatest loss was that the couple got a divorce. They had built their marriage on worldly principles and worldly things. When the storms of life came, their marriage couldn't withstand the pressure. Jesus tells the story of the foolish man and the wise man:

"Therefore everyone who hears these words of mine and puts them into practice is like a wise man who built his house on the rock. The rain came down, the streams rose, and the winds blew and beat against that house; yet it did not fall, because it had its foundation on the rock. But everyone who hears these words of mine and does not put them into practice is like a foolish man who built his house on sand. The rain came down, the streams rose, and the winds blew and beat against that house, and it fell with a great crash." (Matthew 7:24-17)

As couples prepare for marriage, they envision the good side of the marriage vow, health and wealth. In the marriage vow, there is also the side of sickness and poverty. Health and wealth rhyme, but sickness and poverty do not. My hope for each couple who gets married is that they will experience many years of health and wealth. The reality is that the storms of life do come. Couples need to learn how to live with and weather these storms. The key is having a firm foundation. A house built on a good foundation will stand in adversity, while a house with no foundation will fall under pressure. If the couple above would have based their marriage on the

Storms

permanent foundation of Godly principles, rather than worldly, temporal principles, their marriage would have endured. They would have lost all their worldly possessions, but they would still have had what was important, their faith and their marriage.

I knew a man who was successful by worldly standards. He was a self-made millionaire at a very young age. He was seriously injured in an accident. His wife left him. He hired a therapist who was rehabilitating him to strength. The therapist was a wonderful Christian lady. The two fell in love and got married. They have become each other's health and wealth. As God has blessed them in marriage, they have been a blessing to others. We must remember, the same hot water that hardens an egg, is also what softens a bean.

It is not a matter of whether the storms of life come, but rather, when they will come. Storms come in many different forms. There are financial storms, there are sickness storms, and there are relationship storms. Storms come to everyone, but the difference is in our attitude. A Christian attitude has so much to do with understanding the cross of Christ. The cross represents death, destruction, and brokenness; while it also represents resurrection, rebirth, new life, and healing. A Christian understands the reality of life; suffering will come, but there is also healing that takes place. Ultimately, death comes to us, but in Christ there is resurrection from the dead. There is hope in the Christian understanding of life and marriage.

A Christian also has a selfless, servant attitude in life. A Christian is not as concerned about self, as he would be concerned about his wife. A Christian has the perspective of, "What can I put into my marriage, rather than, what can I get out of my marriage?" There are many people who have the attitude, "I want to get something out of life." They will use community only to get out of it what they can. They will use their work to get out of it what they can. This can also be the approach that some take for marriage, "What do I get out of it?" When the storms of life come, a couple will divorce because they have selfish attitudes, rather than a committed servant attitude for each other.

Many couples do not marry, but simply live together. A big reason for this is a lack of commitment. The attitude is, "As long as I am getting things out of this relationship, and my needs are being satisfied, then I will stay in the relationship. As soon as my needs are not being met, then it will be easy to part ways." When a couple has not made the commitment to marry, there are no legal bonds that will prevent them from parting. I remember a couple who was living in a noncommittal relationship, when the man died suddenly at a young age.

Because they were not legally married, she was not entitled to anything that was his. She didn't even qualify for social security benefits.

I knew of another couple who lived together for thirteen years. When the man decided to leave, the woman was entitled to virtually nothing. When the storms of life come, marriage, being legally binding, will protect people. Marriage is an all-or-nothing principle. Either you fully commit to your spouse, or you remain single. Partial commitments in life, whether they be in marriage or otherwise, do not produce the optimal fullness for what God intended. Partial commitments are not godly commitments, and they never work, resulting in a lot of hurt.

God is like an unmovable rock in the middle of a raging river. I think of this rock in the middle of a river as I go canoeing. It is always there. When I was young, I was visiting with a man who was elderly, who also canoed this river as a youth. As I described the rock to him, he knew which one I was referring to. Life is like moving water, so we need a permanent foundation to stand on. God is that firm foundation that will make us withstand the tests of time. A Christian couple will put their faith in Jesus. The Apostle Paul wrote in Romans 5:1-5,

"Therefore, since we have been justified through faith,

we have peace with God through our Lord Jesus Christ, through whom we have gained access by faith into this grace in which we now stand. And we rejoice in the hope of the glory of God. Not only so, but we also rejoice in our sufferings, because we know that suffering produces perseverance, perseverance, character, and character, hope. And hope does not disappoint us, because God has poured out his love into our hearts by the Holy Spirit, whom he has given us."

It is through Jesus Christ that we have access to God. God is with us even in times of suffering. There are three strengths that God gives to us in our suffering. One of those is perseverance. When we have endurance, we can get through the storms of life. The second strength that God gives us is character. Character has to do with attitude. You can have two people who are facing the same problem; one has a good attitude, while the other one has a bad attitude. The one who has the good attitude will get through the tough times much better than the one who does not. The third strength is hope. When people have hope, they have reason to go on in difficult times. When people lose their hope, they will give up. The source of this strength comes by the Holy Spirit, who has been poured into our hearts.

I knew an elderly couple while I was ministering in California in the late 1980's. They were filled with the

Holy Spirit, and showed such a kind disposition to other people. It would be easy to think in their many years of marriage, that things had come easily for them. They shared their story with me about the early years of their marriage. When they got married, they were living in Iowa. They bought a farm, and shortly after, the Great Depression came. They ended up losing their farm. It would have been so easy for them to have parted ways at this point. They got married, and it wasn't long before a great storm came and washed their life of dreams away. He heard a rumor that there was work in southern California. Based on that rumor, they packed what clothes they could into a couple of suitcases, got on a train, and headed for southern California. The rumor was true, there was work for him. He worked as a mason, and made a good living. Together, they were able to raise their family. She told me that she read Psalm 46 before they left Iowa. God gave them strength, courage, hope, and peace, through this psalm. When the storm of life came crashing down on them, God was their refuge and strength, a very present help in trouble. In the death of their early dreams, God gave them a new life in a different place. They are an example of a couple who put their faith in God.

Another story that can give us strength is Jesus calming the storm:

"That day when evening came, he said to his disciples,

The Tie That Binds

'Let us go over to the other side.' Leaving the crowd behind, they took him along, just as he was, in the boat. There were also other boats with him. A furious squall came up, and the waves broke over the boat, so that it was nearly swamped. Jesus was in the stern, sleeping on a cushion. The disciples woke him and said to him, 'Teacher, don't you care if we drown?" He got up, rebuked the wind and said to the waves, 'Quiet! Be still!' Then the wind died down and it was completely calm. He said to his disciples, 'Why are you so afraid? Do you still have no faith?' They were terrified and asked each other, 'Who is this? Even the wind and the waves obey him!'" (Mark 4:35-41)

This story teaches us how abruptly storms can come upon us. Jesus' disciples were experienced fishermen. They knew the Sea of Galilee well. This sea was notorious for its storms that caught people off guard. The sea became so violent that the disciples thought they were perishing. Jesus was in a state of complete peace, as he was fast asleep in the boat. The disciples, who were in anxious desperation, awoke Jesus, thinking he didn't care if they perished. At that point, Jesus commanded the sea to be still.

It is natural to run away from the storms that come upon us. We also do our best to try to prevent storms from

Storms

coming. Even in our best efforts to prevent and run from storms, we sometimes find ourselves in the middle of them. This is where we put our faith in Jesus. Faith is clinging to Jesus in the midst of life. What kept the boat from sinking? Jesus was in it. Jesus is the one who faced the greatest storm of dying on a cross. The storm of death could not destroy Jesus, for he is risen from the dead. We must remember that when Jesus is in our boat, we can sail with the storm. Just when we think that our boat is going to sink, Jesus gives us the strength to get through the storm. We must remember that storms do not last forever. The storms do end; God gives us peace and calm. We must also remember that sometimes God spares us from going through the storms, while other times he allows us to go through the storms. God allows us to go through the storms because it is during these times that he strengthens us. We learn to put our faith in Jesus, who ultimately saves us from death.

When couples live together in a noncommittal relationship, they are doomed to fail because the storms of life will come. Couples who marry, and put their faith in Jesus, will be able to withstand the storms that come. Each time they endure the storms, they gain the strength, the wisdom, and the compassion that only God can give them for life.

Another Bible passage that gives us wisdom and

strength in times of suffering comes from 1 Peter 1:3-9:

"Praise be to the God and Father of our Lord Jesus Christ! In his great mercy he has given us new birth into a living hope through the resurrection of Jesus Christ from the dead, and into an inheritance that can never perish, spoil or fade-kept in heaven for you, who through faith are shielded by God's power until the coming of the salvation that is ready to be revealed in the last time. In this you greatly rejoice, though now for a little while you may have had to suffer grief in all kinds of trials. These have come so that your faith-of greater worth than gold, which perishes even though refined by fire-may be proved genuine and may result in praise, glory and honor when Jesus Christ is revealed. Though you have not seen him, you love him; and even though you do not see him now, you believe in him and are filled with an in expressible and glorious joy, for you are receiving the goal of our faith, the salvation of your souls."

Peter, who wrote this passage, refers to the Christian faith as being more precious than gold. Like gold that is made pure by a refiner's fire, so our faith is made strong through the trials of life. Fire either consumes something, or fire makes it better. Precious metals would be a good example of this. In life, storms can either consume us or they can make us stronger. The storms of life have consumed many people and destroyed many marriages. When we put our faith in God, those storms will make us stronger, and better people. We trust in God who binds us together in love.

I knew a couple where the husband developed a debilitating disease. His wife took care of him for many years. When he reached the advanced stages of his disease, she got cancer and died. This couple was faced with some of the largest storms of life. These storms could have crushed their lives and belief in God. They did not allow these storms to consume them, but rather trusted in God who gave them the strength to live each day for his glory. Their lives displayed joy that only God could give them. God used them as a witness to all who knew them, of the faith that endures the sufferings of this life. Their lives were filled with the faith that made them well. It was this faith that kept them ever vigilant of the eternal life that God has promised them in Jesus Christ.

The Tie That Binds

STUDY QUESTIONS

1. What types of storms have you faced in life?
2. Is your marriage commitment strong enough to care for your spouse in times of debilitating injury or disease? How are you being each other's health and wealth?
3. What does it mean to have a servant attitude in marriage?
4. How do the storms of life make you stronger?
5. What is changing in your world? How do you understand Jesus as being your stability in a changing world?
6. What Bible story best illustrates God being your help in the storms of life?

12

IMAGING

An image is our mental picture of something or someone. Sometimes people can paint or draw a picture of the image, or a person can make a sculpted image.

Imagine is trying to develop a mental picture of how something might be. An image is our mental picture of something, while imagine is what we would like the mental picture to be.

"So God created man in his own image; in the image of God he created him; male and female he created them." (Genesis 1:27) People are created in God's image. Nobody has seen God, so are we to say that somewhere out there God is a human? As people, are we created in the physical image of God, or is it a more virtuous image? Nobody has seen God, so it is hard to have a physical image of God to model, and if we are to live in a virtuous image, that has been lost in the fall of sin.

We are not to make any graven images of the Lord. "You shall not make for yourself an idol in the form of anything in heaven above or on the earth beneath or in the waters below." (Exodus 20:4) If we are created in the image of God, how do we know what that image looks like, much less make an image of it? That is the danger of making an image of God, is that we are making God to be what he isn't. The Apostle Paul helps us to better understand the image of God:

"He (Jesus) is the image of the invisible God, the firstborn over all creation. For by him all things were created: things in heaven and on earth, visible and invisible, whether thrones or powers or rulers or authorities; all things were created by him and for him. He is before all things, and in him all things hold together. And he is the head of the body, the church; he is the beginning and the firstborn from among the dead, so that in everything he might have the supremacy. For God was pleased to have all his fullness dwell in him, and through him to reconcile to himself all things, whether things on earth or things in heaven, by making peace through his

Imaging

blood, shed on the cross." (Colossians 1:15-20)

Jesus is the image of God in all of God's fullness. If we want to know what God looks like, acts like, and his character, we study the life of Jesus Christ. God, who is hidden and veiled behind creation, has become revealed to us in Jesus Christ. Jesus Christ is risen from the dead, and is present in the Holy Spirit. The Holy Spirit dwells in the believers, the church. If people are looking for the image of Jesus in our world today, the church is the image. The church is the body of Christ, where Jesus is the head.

John writes, "Dear friends, let us love one another, for love comes from God. Everyone who loves has been born of God and knows God. Whoever does not love does not know God, because God is love. This is how God showed his love among us: He sent his one and only Son into the world that we might live through him. This is love: not that we loved God, but that he loved us and sent his Son as an atoning sacrifice for our sins. Dear friends, since God so loved us, we also ought to love one another. No one has ever seen God; but if we love one another; God lives in us and his love is made complete in us." (1 John 4:7-12)

When we are loved by God, we live in his image. When we love others, we show the image of God to others. The church is to be the image of God's love working in the world. When we find our value living in God's love and acceptance, when we accept ourselves, and when we love others, we live in the image of God. This is the image God created us to be in. We want to live in the image of God.

The world has its image for us. This image is very different than the one God has for us. An example of the world's image is the Barbie and Ken dolls. Children begin playing with these dolls at a young age. The world will say that Barbie is the perfect female image, and Ken is the perfect image of a male. As children play with these dolls, they connect with them, thinking this is how they are to look or will look someday. As children grow older, they realize that they are not in the image of a Barbie and Ken doll, and this is a crushing blow to their self-image. The world accepts us when we look like Barbie and Ken dolls. When we are less than this image, the world says, "You're not good enough." We have trouble accepting ourselves, when we realize that we are not in the image of Barbie and Ken dolls. People will suffer from eating disorders, depression, and will go to extreme lengths to try to live in the image of Barbie and Ken. When it comes to our physical self, the world will tell us we are too tall, too short, our hair isn't the right color, and our complexion isn't appealing enough. Mentally, the world

Imaging

will tell us that we are not intelligent enough. The world would want us at an A level, so a C or D level is not acceptable.

As Christian couples, we are to find our individual acceptance and the acceptance for each other through the love of God. If we are looking for acceptance on worldly principles, we will always fall short of those expectations. None of us can live up to the image of Barbie and Ken. They are pretend people. Unfortunately, we develop pretend people. We would like to marry Barbie or Ken, because in our imagination they are the perfect people.

In marriage, we are to love and accept our spouse on the basis of God's love. We marry the person for whom he is, understanding that he has his flaws. You don't say, "Once we get married, I will change him or her." We don't marry someone in hopes of transforming him into our pretend person. We don't marry someone thinking they are going to be our lifetime project; acting like we are a potter and the person we have married is our clay to mold. This makes a person frustrated because how one's spouse goes about making his/her spouse in one's image is through criticism, nitpicking, and comparing them to other people. As couples marry, they must be at the place where they say, "This is the person I know, love, and accept. I do not want him to be anybody else."

I will ask couples who are preparing for marriage,

The Tie That Binds

"What are five things you like about the person you are marrying? These are five attractions that tell your spouse, "I admire you." This is also an affirmation of their person, giving acceptance of whom he/she is.

I will say to couples, "You are marrying the perfect person, but tell me one to three imperfections of this perfect person?" The reason for this exercise is to let one's spouse know that there are some things that I don't like, but I'm not going to let them destroy our marriage. I accept you for who you are in spite of these imperfections, and I'm not going to spend the rest of our lives nagging you about them.

This is a gross analogy, but it illustrates this point. I remember a woman who shared that she didn't like her fiancé chewing tobacco. She went out and bought him an engraved spittoon. This was her way of communicating to him, "I love you for who you are, and I'm not going to let your tobacco habit get in the way of a special marriage."

My story is one of dirty socks. This would be one of my many imperfections. I leave dirty socks on the bedroom floor. After my wife tried to tell me to pick up my socks to no avail, she got me a dirty laundry basket to place my socks in. When she still noticed socks on the floor, she said, "I understand that you once played basketball. Let's have a competition, I'll take one sock and you take the other, and we will see who can make the

Imaging

basket first." Instead of getting upset with me, she was creative to make a game of it. Instead of fighting with your spouse, use humor and creativity to make your point.

You cannot rely on someone else to make you happy. Joy comes by having the Holy Spirit dwelling within us. Your inner spiritual joy will have a positive effect on others and will be of strength to your marriage.

You cannot control another person, but you can control yourself. You cannot control how another person acts, but you can control how you react. I took a group of youth to New York City on a mission trip. One evening, I took the group to see a New York Yankees baseball game. It was a wonderful experience, although the people sitting behind me were drinking alcoholic beverages throughout the game, and by the seventh inning were being obnoxious. I was starting to feel perturbed by their vulgar language, then I had thoughts of their spilling beer on me. I thought, "If they baptize me with their beer, I will not be happy and someone is going to hurt." I made up my mind that this would be my reaction. In that moment, I prayed. God calmed my emotions, and I thought about this. If I start a fist fight with these people, I would be escorted out by the police. In that event, I would wait outside the stadium and meet the rest of the group when they exited at the end of the game. Then I started to think about the example I would be for the youth, and that is not to say that they would just escort me out of the stadium. Maybe I would have to spend the night in jail. That would really put our group in a predicament. Finally, I decided that if I get beer dumped down my head and back, my reaction would be to sit there, humiliated. So when another person acts inappropriately, including your spouse, it is good to think ahead of time how you will respond in different circumstances.

As we marry someone for who he or she is, we must also be ourselves. There are some people who will be a pretend person in their dating, only to change after they are married. It is disillusionment, when a person realizes that they are not married to the person they were dating. A person can impress another person by being someone he is not through stories about himself that are not true. They will be charming when in the presence of this person, but otherwise is not. The person they are pretending to be through their stories and charm is a false one. This is why a longer courtship with someone you haven't known very long is important. In time, a person's true self will be revealed.

Another problem in marriage is spouses that are controlling. They do not respect their spouse for who they are, but rather try to make them to be a pretend person through criticism, manipulation, and coercion. They want their spouses to be programmed like a remote control.

Imaging

Relationships are based on love. Love allows our spouses to have the freedom to be themselves.

When your spouse is controlling, you need to confront the person and their controlling behavior. People control when they have low self-esteem, are insecure, and are unsure of themselves. They will often try to control their spouses because they have no control of the rest of their lives, and they feel empowered by dictating to their spouses how to live. This is where a person needs to confront the controlling person. Controlling people do not like to be confronted. When confronted, they often back down. One way to confront a controlling person is to respond to their statement by saying, "What?" This way you are not receiving the critical remarks, you make the person think again about what he is saying, and you are not agreeing with what he has said or done.

A second way is by saying, "You will not treat me this way." You have respect for yourself, and you will not allow that to be violated. You have set personal boundaries that you will not compromise for any reason. If your spouse does not have respect for your boundaries, then you need to go to a higher authority that will enforce those boundaries for you.

A third way is to state your name. State who you are as a person. Then you need to ask the controlling person, "Name the person you want me to be." Or, "Who do you want this pretend person to be?" You conclude by saying, "I am who I am, and I will not be this pretend person you want me to be."

In marriage, you do not want to make mountains out of mole hills. This is where little things, can become big issues. If you are a night person, and your spouse is a morning person, you need to show sensitivity to each other. You need to compromise the night and morning in a way that will allow your schedules to compliment rather than conflict with each other. Conflicts arise when a woman would like to be with her husband at evening social functions, and she is hurt when he accuses her of sleeping in late and not being good for anything. When this happens, it is important to state your positive case for being a morning or night person. Your spouse is not to take it personally, and then tell your spouse how much you love him or her. It is important to say to your spouse why you want him or her to be involved in your life, even though you have different schedules.

It is a challenge when you are an orderly person, and your spouse is messy. She likes everything neat and in their places, while he operates out of what he calls an organized mess. When this occurs, it is important to designate your spaces. For an orderly wife to say, "The kitchen is my space and it will be clean," her husband will need to respect it. When a husband allows a messy shop,

Imaging

this is his domain and she shouldn't worry about it.

You may want to use your vacation time to travel, while your spouse wants to stay at home. This is where a couple needs to work on compromises. If they both get two weeks of vacation a year, the one week could be a traveling vacation, while the other week is a stay at home vacation. Both need to work on how this will be a special time for both of them. The main thing about a vacation is that you are together, whether that be at home or some other place. When you are together, that is the most special vacation.

It is important to recognize that mole hills exist. We are not looking to remove mole hills, but we want to work with them in a way that will prevent them from becoming mountains.

STUDY QUESTIONS

1. What images do you have in life for God? For people? For your spouse?
2. What are things that you try to imagine?
3. Do you see Jesus as the image of God? Do you imagine Jesus as the image of humanity?
4. We may try to live in the image of Barbie and Ken dolls. What other images does the world want you to conform to?
5. If you were to create a pretend person, what would the person look like? What kind of personality would this person have?
6. What are five imperfections about your spouse? What are five things you like about your spouse?
7. What mountains have you created from mole hills?

BIBLIOGRAPHY

Bible, New International version.

Evans, Patricia. *Controlling People* (Avon, Massachusetts: Adams Media, 2002).

Fruzzetti, Alan. *The High-Conflict Couple* (Oakland, CA: New Harbinger Publications, Inc., 2006).

Gottman, John. *Why Marriages Succeed or Fail* (New York, New York: Simon & Schuster, 1994).

Gray, John. *Men Are From Mars, Women Are From Venus* (New York, New York: Harper Collins, 1992).

Harley, Jr., Willard F. *His Needs Her Needs* (Grand Rapids, MI: Baker Book House Company, 1994).

Lewis, C. S. *The Four Loves* (New York, New York: Harcourt Bace, 1960).

Smalley, Gary. *Making Love Last Forever* (Dallas, TX: Word Publishing, 1996).

Also from Baal Hamon Publishers:

Worship That Pleases God - by James W. Bartley, Jr. (PhD)
February 2008, 360 pages, 6' x 9'
ISBN 9780756884 (Paperback: US $17.99, UK £13.99)
Category: Non-fiction

James W. Bartley Jr. has gone beyond the common status quo to explore a subject that most authors do not have sufficient experiential credentials to delve into. He practically reflects on his more than 60 years experience of walking with God to bring many into an awe-striking deeper communion with God. His book, Worship that pleases God gives an accurate insight into the inexhaustible subject of Worship – as an invaluable asset in the Man-God relationship. Being a retired Professor of theology, Dr. Bartley has successfully made a holistic and unassailable exposition of worship – as a theme that finds its root in the book of Genesis and continues to Revelation in the Bible, while his academic perception lends credence to his work. Worship that pleases God is not just a book that enriches the knowledge of inquisitive readers; Dr. Bartley has carefully sequenced it in such a manner that even the least motivated reader will simply find the wave of his discovered supernatural worship pattern so irresistible.

Order from www.baalhamon.com

Also from Baal Hamon Publishers:

The Fatherless – a novel by Erin Inman
February 2008, 420 pages, 5.5' x 8.5'
ISBN 9780756914 (Paperback: US $17.99, UK £13.99)
Category: Fiction

Nick Pierce, a talented young boy whose singular obsession is music, finds himself overturned from a lonely life with his grandmother in Wichita, Kansas to the rather strange atmosphere of life in Western Kansas with the father he had never met. Although a friendly neighbor couple takes Nick under their wing, circumstances in life and his father's attitude work against him. In search for a way to fulfill his uttermost desires, he enters into a world of the unknown – a stranger world that leads him into questioning right from wrong. In the face of a life-threatening sickness, Nick wonders if life could offer him a little more, if music may still flow from his fingers, in praise to the Father-God.

Order from www.baalhamon.com

Also from Baal Hamon Publishers:
Take Me Home Windrider – by Jeff Knighton
July 2010, 264 pages, 5.5' x 8.5'
ISBN 9784956500 (Paperback: US $15.99)
Category: Non-fiction

God uses nature to teach us His ways. God has taught Dr. Knighton to be a true Christian from his uniquely rich experience as a ranch hand in Texas. It was there that he enjoyed the tough but fulfilling labors of working with horses and cattle. The work offered plenty of hours under the deep Texan sky, in both kind and harsh weather, to examine his own spirit as he rode pasture observing nature, and tending to the cattle under his watch. This book captures the reflections that have given Dr. Knighton a perspective on life unique to those who have been privileged to spend time as a working cowboy which over the years has enhanced his work as a teacher and preacher. These reflections have been used as discussion starters in small group Bible studies, and as illustrations in preaching. They afford the reader an adventurous ride in the inner man with Christ.

Order from www.baalhamon.com

Also from Baal Hamon Publishers:

Does God Truly Exist? – by Temitope Oyetomi
August 2006, 360 pages, 6' x 9'
ISBN 9780756825 (Paperback: US $17.99)
Category: Non-fiction

Archbishop Akinola, Primate of the Church of Nigeria (Anglican Communion) 2000 – 2010, commends this book as a "valuable material for anyone tired of dodging the questions". Indeed, it is one book that has "raised a fathom of questions", as yet another Bishop - a PhD-holder - observes in the foreword. However, the tact with which the author resolves many of these questions is scholarly and engaging. The author writes with confidence and his arguments are intelligent and highly persuasive: facts and their interpretations are presented in a style that is approachable, digestible and amenable to reading by a wide audience. Ordinarily, one might think of it as a book for those who are in doubt of God's existence. Of course, it is. But it will be more applicable to those who are sure that God exists and who believe they are worshiping the true and living God. "Who really is the true and living God" and "how best can one relate with God" are the ultimate quests of the book. Drawing answers from science, religion and philosophy, the author has contrived a rare blend "that will plausibly challenge every mind". No wonder a Baptist minister recommends it "to all people no matter their religious persuasions". It is certainly an intellectual masterpiece.

Also from Baal Hamon Publishers:

Fellow Nigerians, I Wish You Good Luck – by Temitope Oyetomi
March 2011, 160 pages, 5' x 8'
ISBN 9784956519 (Paperback: US $7.99)
Category: Non-fiction

Is there a real connection between cleverness, good governance and good luck? The answer may not be so simple and direct. That is why the author of this book an experienced editor has painstakingly ploughed through anecdotes, news, history, and reasoning to blend a masterful piece that manages to be funny, witty, pragmatic and eye-opening all at once. The primary foci of the book are issues relating to the 2011 presidential elections in Nigeria but the book goes on to open up a typical Nigerian soul in an uncommonly down-to-earth manner.

Nigeria is Africa s most populous country, often touted as the Giant of Africa and Heart of Africa . The incumbent president goes by the first name Goodluck a name which has seemingly always put him in the right places at the right times over the years. Would the Nigerian nation be electing a harbinger of good fortunes if they elect him as president in 2011? This crazy book broaches on that sensitive question whilst dwelling more on extant issues that perennially afflict the Heart of Africa and relentlessly taunt the Giant of Africa.

Also from Baal Hamon Publishers:

Stop Arguing With Me– by Duane Cuthbertson
July 2011, 160 pages, 5' x 8'
ISBN 9784956578 (Paperback: US $7.99)
Category: Non-fiction

The need for this book is epidemic. Media outlets daily "scream" with incidents of anger and domestic violence. National and International tensions surround us. Is it possible to discern the source of such wrath? The author will share with you that the "human spirit" can be "crushed" and "fractured". Both generic temperament and environmental factors can lead to this manifestation. The book will have little value for you unless you at some time in your life have argued or been in tension with others. However, if this does include you, the author will give you not only hope but also a technique for healing. May we all indeed come to a point where the "peace of God can rule in our hearts . . . " (Colossians 3: 15).

www.ingramcontent.com/pod-product-compliance
Lightning Source LLC
LaVergne TN
LVHW091259080426
835510LV00007B/322